DR. TONI GRANT, distinguished psychologist
and star of the award-winning radio talk
show "The Dr. Toni Grant Program,"
challenges and exposes
THE TEN BIG LIES OF LIBERATION

LIE #1   YOU CAN HAVE IT ALL.

LIE #2   MEN AND WOMEN ARE
            FUNDAMENTALLY THE SAME.

LIE #3   DESIRABILITY IS ENHANCED BY
            ACCOMPLISHMENT.

LIE #4   YOUR FULL POTENTIAL *MUST* BE
            REALIZED.

LIE #5   MEN AND WOMEN VIEW SEX IN THE
            SAME WAY.

LIE #6   MOTHERHOOD CAN BE POSTPONED
            WITHOUT PENALTY.

LIE #7   TODAY'S WOMAN SHOULD ABANDON
            "SOFTNESS" FOR "ASSERTIVENESS."

LIE #8   SPEAKING ONE'S MIND IS BETTER
            THAN LISTENING.

LIE #9   A WOMAN DOESN'T NEED A MAN
            EXCEPT FOR BREEDING.

LIE #10   A WOMAN SHOULD LOOK FOR
            SENSITIVITY, NOT STRENGTH, IN
            A MAN.

FROM DR. TONI GRANT— THE FOUR ASPECTS OF WOMAN

DO YOU RECOGNIZE YOURSELF?

The Madonna embodies the quintessential feminine virtues of patience, silence, and faith. She does not seek to attain greatness for herself—rather she inspires the man in her life to greatness, supporting him unconditionally in his quest for fulfillment and achievement.

The Mother is caretaker, a woman who thrives upon her attachments to others. She nurtures not only her own children, but other relatives and friends, as well as the men in her life.

The Amazon is highly focused, ambitious, assertive, goal-oriented, and self-sufficient. She relates to the men in her life as companions, co-workers, and competitors.

The Courtesan relates to a man on intellectual and emotional as well as sexual levels. She sings a kind of harmony to her man, but she is not subservient to him. The Courtesan is an aspect of woman which men have adored through the ages.

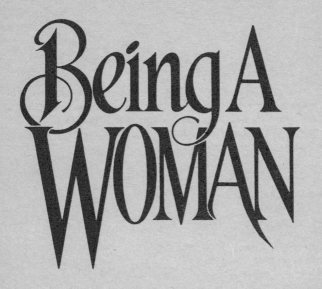

Being A WOMAN

FULFILLING YOUR FEMININITY AND FINDING LOVE

DR. TONI GRANT

AVON BOOKS  NEW YORK

Grateful acknowledgment is made to Twentieth Century-Fox Film Corporation for permission to reprint a monologue by Bette Davis as Margot Channing from the motion picture *All About Eve*. Copyright 1951, renewed 1977, Twentieth Century-Fox Film Corporation. Used by permission. All rights reserved.

AVON BOOKS
A division of
The Hearst Corporation
105 Madison Avenue
New York, New York 10016

Copyright © 1988 by Toni G. Grant, Ph.D., Psychologist, Inc.
Inside cover author photograph copyright © 1988 by Harry Langdon Photography
Published by arrangement with Random House, Inc.
Library of Congress Catalog Card Number: 87-9667
ISBN: 0-380-70698-9

First Avon Books Printing: June 1989

AVON TRADEMARK REG. U.S. PAT. OFF. AND IN OTHER COUNTRIES, MARCA REGISTRADA, HECHO EN U.S.A.

Printed in the U.S.A.

K–R   10   9   8   7   6   5   4   3   2   1

To my mother,
Blanche Walker Grant,
my greatest inspiration

Ad astra per aspera

—ATTRIBUTED TO SENECA

Funny business, a woman's career, the things you drop on your way up the ladder so you can move faster. You forget you need them again when you get back to being a woman. That's one career all females have in common, whether we like it or not: Being a woman. Sooner or later we've got to work at it, no matter how many other careers we've had or wanted. And in the last analysis, nothing's any good unless you can look up just before dinner or turn around in bed, and there he is. Without that, you're not a woman. You're something with a French Provincial office or a book full of clippings. But you're not a woman.

—BETTE DAVIS in *All About Eve*

PREFACE

This is a book about love, as are many women's books. Women are passionately concerned about love, involved in it, and in search of it. Love is a female preoccupation, more the business of women than of men. This book will make a strong case for the validity of this preoccupation and for the psychological and biological differences between the sexes.

On my daily radio program on the Mutual Broadcasting System, I talk to diverse types of women from all across the country: rural areas to urban centers, varying income brackets, different levels of education, across a wide range in age, approximately eighteen to sixty, with most in their twenties, thirties, and early forties. Most of these women have jobs or careers (their work varies greatly, from a woman who worked in a plant to a Ph.D. in medieval history), but they don't call to ask me about their work; they call to ask me about men.

In general, the women I speak with don't have trouble getting men, but they do have trouble getting— and staying—married. They want me to tell them what to *do* about this. But getting married does not so much demand that a woman *do* something, but rather that she *be* in the right frame of mind for *bonding* with a man.

This frame of mind can be characterized as a uniquely feminine attitude, a particular way of being a woman. But the modern woman has denounced and suppressed this way of being in the world and now needs to be encouraged to embrace her lost femininity; specifically, the Mother, Madonna, and Courtesan aspects of her personality. This shift in consciousness can be a frightening and difficult one for the woman of today, for she has become an Amazon Woman, out of touch with her softer nature. This new Amazon Woman must now learn to integrate her newfound identity as a person of accomplishment with her needs for love and feminine fulfillment.

Many of the stories in this book are composites of case histories of patients seen in my private practice; other examples have been distilled from the many stories told to me nightly on the radio. All case histories have been modified so that the anonymity of those who have so generously shared their most private thoughts and feelings will be protected.

ACKNOWLEDGMENTS

My warmest thanks to Susan Block for her collaboration on this manuscript. Her enthusiastic support of the material and her tireless energies greatly facilitated the writing process and made this a journey filled with laughter and love.

Being a Woman is the culmination of several years of research and study in an area of consuming interest to me. My intellectual debts are enormous; the many scholars who influenced my thinking are listed in the bibliography, and I am most grateful to them. I felt a sense of mounting excitement as I read these works and developed the theories that are presented in this book. On a personal level, this process transformed me, as I hope my readers will be transformed. In writing *Being a Woman*, I became more of a woman, and for this I am especially grateful.

There are many people to thank for supporting my vision, among them:

Howard Kaminsky, former publisher of Random House, who sent me flowers and encouraged me to write a "passionate book";
Kate Medina, my brilliantly talented editor at Random House, who modulated my tone and guided my hand with a tact and tenacity truly characteristic of an "Amazon Lady"—a woman of sweetness and of strength;
Suzanne Wickham, West Coast publicity director of Random House, for her warmth, friendship, and support of the project;

Dr. Patricia Allen, for introducing me to the work of C. G. Jung and his followers;

Dr. Arnold P. Goldstein, professor of psychology, Syracuse University, for teaching me that psychology is for the many, not the few;

Dr. Robert Goulding and Mary McClure Goulding, for introducing me to transactional analysis and the concept of the "life script";

Raymond Katz, my personal manager, and his associate, Eric Gold, for guiding my career with skill and care;

Ben Hoberman and Bruce Marr, for first opening the doors of radio broadcasting to me and believing in the value of "media psychology";

Norman Pattiz, chairman of the board, CEO, Westwood One/Mutual Broadcasting System, for recently affording me the opportunity of developing and exploring these ideas on the radio airwaves;

Steve Sohmer, my friend, for sharing with me the pleasures and pain of writing.

Others who must be thanked include Janice Miller, my longtime personal secretary, for locating reference and research materials, and for her patience and faith; Richard Chavez, my radio producer, for cheerfully photocopying many copies of the book, and Olga Tarnowski, assistant to Kate Medina.

Without my family none of this would be possible. I would like to express my love and gratitude to: Blanche Walker Grant, my mother, a remarkable woman, whose confidence in me has been a source of strength all the days of my life;

Dr. Joseph Grant, my father, a truly "Good Man" of impeccable integrity, who fought my battles for me when I couldn't fight them for myself;

Dr. Barry Grant, my brother, whose caring and friendship have been a consistent source of comfort;

Dr. Neil Hollander, the father of my children, for allowing me to grow;

Kimberly Anne Hollander, my daughter, for her understanding heart and gentle soul;

Courtney Grant Hollander, my daughter, for her patience and love throughout the long hours of my writing.

Finally, a warm embrace to my radio listeners, whose presence is unseen but deeply felt, and to the thousands of callers who have honored and trusted me by sharing their most intimate thoughts and feelings. You have enriched my life, enhanced my self-esteem, broadened my horizons, and helped me feel loved. For this, and much more, I thank you.

December 1987   —T.G.G.

CONTENTS

INTRODUCTION

Being a woman is much more than simply being female. Womanhood has been a mystery throughout the ages, fascinating and baffling to even the most learned amongst us. Sigmund Freud, late in his career, is said to have despaired, "What do women want?" In 1932, a student of Freud's named C. G. Jung wrote, "It is a foregone conclusion among the initiated that men understand nothing of women's psychology as it actually is, but it is astonishing to find that women do not know themselves."[1]

Perhaps the feminine psyche will always remain elusive, a mystery to both men and women. But one thing is certain: In the last decade, feminine consciousness has changed. Never before in history have women asked so much of themselves, of their men, and of life. "Having it all" has become the prevailing ethic and expectation of the modern female. Being a woman in the twentieth century would appear to be a whole new game—or is it? Despite our efforts toward androgyny, could there be an essence of femininity that has always existed and always will, a quintessential difference between the sexes?

Several years ago, I began a systematic study of feminine psychology. I combed the literature in an effort to find a theory which would express what it means to be a woman. I wanted a theory that would speak to the heart of the mother, the career woman, the wife, and the mistress. I wanted a theory in which Everywoman could see herself and ultimately find herself. Eventually I discovered the compelling work of Carl Jung and his associates.

Jung believed that within every woman is a "man," and within every man is a "woman." He called the feminine aspect of man the "anima" and the masculine aspect of woman the "animus." He felt that in order to be fully realized human beings, to be whole, both men and women needed, in the course of a lifetime, to integrate the male and the female within.

Jungian psychology is complex; it deals with the spirit as well as with the mind, with love as well as with logic. I make no apology for my efforts to simplify this elegant and moving body of literature, for my book is written not for the scholar or for the professional analyst, but for every woman who wants a heightened understanding of her life—and for every man who wants an expanded awareness of his woman.

CHAPTER ONE

The Big Lies of Liberation: Modern Woman Led Astray

Today's woman is an imitation man, at war with actual men, confused and unsettled by it. The contemporary American woman is an Amazon Woman, and she is a product of her times. Her strengths and her weaknesses, what she has gained and what she has lost, are in large part the subject of this book.

At its inception, the feminist movement, accompanied by the sexual revolution, made a series of enticing, exciting promises to women. These promises sounded good, so good that many women deserted their men and their children or rejected the entire notion of marriage and family, in pursuit of "themselves" and a career. These pursuits, which emphasized self-sufficiency and individualism, were supposed to enhance a woman's quality of life and improve her options, as well as her relations with men. Now, a decade or so later, women have had to face the fact that, in many ways, feminism and liberation made promises that could not be delivered.

Many a modern woman is now desperate to rediscover that which she has lost—call it femininity, the power of relatedness, or what you will. Let us examine, then, some of the cruel myths and unfulfilled promises propagated by the more extreme elements of the feminist and sexual revolutions. I call these

1

myths quite simply "The big lies of liberation," for the delusional impact of these lies upon the consciousness of the American woman has been substantial and should not be prettied up with fancy psychological terms.

BIG LIE NUMBER ONE: HAVING IT ALL

Even Simone de Beauvoir, renowned feminist author of *The Second Sex*, did not attempt to have it all. According to de Beauvoir, it was "the baby or the book,"[1] and that was that. Contemporary movements led women to believe that they had an endless reservoir of physical and psychic energy, and, of course, they don't. Just like men, women are only human. The woman who focuses her energy into shaping a brilliant career has that much less left over to improve her relationships, to support her man, and to raise her children. Yet many women today devalue their unique contribution as women vis-à-vis their families. The woman who uses her intellect and her energies in support of her man and her family as opposed to her own self-fulfillment via a career is thought to be a fool, underdeveloped, somehow inadequate. Feminism has said not only that women *can* do what men do, but that women *ought* to do what men do. Since men simply can't do what women do (have children), this forces the contemporary woman to do a kind of superhuman double duty that often leaves her exhausted and ineffective. This is, in essence, the bitter dilemma of the contemporary woman. She may have gained the whole world—or at least a place in it—but the price she has had to pay often feels like the loss of her very soul.

BIG LIE NUMBER TWO: ANDROGYNY

This is the belief that men and women are fundamentally the same. This isn't true. Men and women are not only biologically and anatomically different, they are psychologically different as well. It is universally observed that women seem more complex than men, more mysterious, more changeable, more intuitive, more interested in love and relationship. To suggest, as de Beauvoir and others have, that these differences are entirely cultural is absurd. In *In a Different Voice*, Harvard clinical psychologist Carol Gilligan discusses at great length the multitude of studies which have investigated and observed the playground behavior of young boys and girls.[2] The studies selected clearly indicate consistently different behavior patterns between the boys and the girls. Young boys play by rules or agreed-upon principles, and adherence to these principles is considered extremely important. Breaking of the rules is considered a cardinal offense and grounds for exclusion from the group. Girls, however, make few rules and seldom actually play by the few they do make. They are more attuned to feelings; that is, they want to make everyone feel good and be happy. The principles or rules by which little girls live are rules of relatedness; that is, rules that have to do with how people get along with one another. To put it simply: Little girls—and grown women—care more about love than they do about law. This is the essence of being a woman.

BIG LIE NUMBER THREE: DESIRABILITY IS ENHANCED BY ACCOMPLISHMENT

This lie suggested that a woman's attractiveness to men would increase with her achievements. Many women believed in this myth of self-improvement, only to find that it led to competition with men—competition that was appropriate in the business world, but inappropriate in the realm of the personal. Many a contemporary woman approaches a man as yet another test to be taken, another trophy to be won.

Somehow, the idea prevailed that professional accomplishments and increased power in the world would lead to even greater desirability by men. What the liberation movements of the sixties and seventies did not address or even seem to understand was just what it was that men truly appreciated and cherished in women. Men certainly do admire and respect accomplished women, just as they admire and respect accomplished men. Yet in male-female relationships of a personal nature, different drives and needs are operative. In love, a woman is adored and cherished not only for her accomplishments, but for her unique feminine attributes. These attributes involve values of love, relatedness, inspiration, and spirituality.

Often the contemporary woman is shocked and profoundly disappointed that her hard-won accomplishments have not resulted in the male devotion and the improved relationship between the sexes that feminism promised her. The contemporary woman did not anticipate that being overeducated might hamper her ability to relate to men. Yet research statistics indicate that the higher a woman's education, the less apt she is to marry and the fewer appropriate partners she will have from which to choose.[3] Simply put, it is a "Big Lie" that men will lust after or greatly desire a woman because she is highly educated. Formal education may be an asset in the marketplace, but in matters of the heart it can be a liability.

BIG LIE NUMBER FOUR: THE MYTH OF ONE'S "UNREALIZED POTENTIAL"

This is the erroneous belief that we all have tremendous potential that simply *must* be realized. All of us do, in fact, have unrealized potential. But very few people have the drive and motivation to actualize even a part of it, much less all of it. The contemporary woman has fallen prey to the cruel myth that she is "special," one of the few, when the probability is that she is ordinary and one of the many. Many women today suffer from what is known as "grandiosity," the belief that one is far more important than one really is. Psychologically, this is an inflation of the self, a disturbance in the accurate perception of one's personal reality.

The modern woman thus expends tremendous amounts of physical and psychic energy in the working world, yet is often disappointed by her lack of professional growth and life satisfaction. This is sometimes due to sexism; often, however, it is due to the simple fact that most women are ordinary people—just like most men. And, just like most men, today's average woman is just another cog in the wheel of the work force, with a rather low probability of ever becoming president of the company.

BIG LIE NUMBER FIVE: SEXUAL SAMENESS

This lie of liberation, largely perpetrated by the sexual revolution, is particularly devastating in that it suggests that men and women are capable of enjoying sex in the same way. In reality, most women simply cannot separate sex from love as easily as men can. Casual sex leaves most women feeling sad and unfulfilled. Freud was right: Biology is destiny. Contraception notwithstanding, some things never change; we cannot transform the nature of life itself. It is still "nine minutes for him, nine months for her." With every act of sexual intercourse, a woman may be facing a potential new life. Sexual intercourse remains an act of profound significance for a woman, for she carries within her the possibility of bearing new life. This is an undeniable reality of being female; that is, a woman carries the physical and psychic apparatus for the reproduction of the species within herself. The lie of sexual equality has led to widespread promiscuity among women, detachment from their bodies, and indeed, from their very souls.

BIG LIE NUMBER SIX: THE DENIAL OF MATERNITY

The contemporary woman's refusal to accept the inevitability of aging has led to the widespread postponement of marriage and children in the interest of pursuing individuality and solidifying career goals. This approach to life completely denies the reality of a woman's reproductive system and the limitations of time. Recent medical research has substantiated what we have all long suspected: Childbearing in the over-age woman has many liabilities for both mother and child. Once again, it is not so much a question as to whether motherhood *can* be postponed, but whether it *should* be postponed. Those ovaries don't go on forever, and today's over-thirty-five woman often finds herself in a panic in her desperate and unexpected race against time. Thinking she could be "young forever," she wakes up one morning to find she is only human, and getting older.

BIG LIE NUMBER SEVEN: TO BE "FEMININE" IS TO BE WEAK

This lie denies the *power* of femininity. Traditional feminine behaviors—softness, sweetness, kindness, and relatedness—were often viewed as downright ridiculous. The girlish exuberance which comes so naturally to most women was discarded in favor of male aggressiveness. In reality, feminine "soft" behaviors are tremendously powerful and hypnotically appealing both to men and to women. These behaviors greatly enhance a woman's feelings of vulnerability, receptivity, and desirability; these feelings, in turn, inspire high levels of devotion and protection from men. Many a "liberated woman" failed to recognize that men respond most favorably to behaviors in women which are *different* from their own, not the same. The contemporary woman's newly acquired masculine skills in assertiveness may be effective in the marketplace, but they often prove uncomfortable and destructive for both men and women in personal relationships. Many women today don't even seem to know *how* to operate in a feminine modality, and, at this point, they need to be taught.

BIG LIE NUMBER EIGHT: DOING IS BETTER THAN BEING

That is, activity is better than passivity, expressivity better than receptivity. In other words, speaking one's mind is better than listening and being silent. Traditional feminine behaviors do involve a type of passive receptivity and silence. These behaviors have been devalued by feminism as demeaning to women and ineffective in the world. While there is some truth to the contention that passive receptivity is not a powerful tool in the external world, it is a deeply appreciated aspect of woman in the world of love. To listen, to be there, to receive the other with an open heart and mind—this has always been one of the most vital roles of woman. Most women do this quite naturally, but many have come to feel uneasy in this role. Instead, they work frantically on assertiveness, aggression, personal expression, and power, madly suppressing their feminine instincts of love and relatedness.

BIG LIE NUMBER NINE: THE MYTH OF SELF-SUFFICIENCY

One might recall here the famous feminist slogan "A woman needs a man like a fish needs a bicycle." Attempts at self-sufficiency, sexual and otherwise, are hallmarks of Amazon thinking, not just in contemporary American society, but in ancient mythology. In the legendary Amazon culture, the Amazons lived an entirely female existence in which they functioned without men. Once a year, the women who participated in breeding would go to neighboring islands, meet the most desirable and virile males, and return alone to their own island to bear the children. The female children were kept and raised in the Amazon society; the male children were returned to the societies whence they came. American society is not quite at this point. In this past decade, however, it has not been uncommon to hear contemporary women refer to men as "studs"; in other words, good for nothing more than mating and breeding. And often, when I ask a modern woman exactly what she needs a man for, "breeding" seems to be her primary answer.

BIG LIE NUMBER TEN: THAT WOMEN WOULD ENJOY THE FEMINIZATION OF MEN

As women embraced more masculine values and men more feminine values, we thought we would enjoy each other all the more. In fact, the contemporary "soft male" (otherwise known as "The New Wimp") has been brutally denigrated by women, and the search for the Macho Man is on. Women are yearning for something, they know not what, but they are beginning to suspect that it has something to do with being a "real woman" again, involved with a "real man."

Few men actually want to go back to the old-fashioned fifties male, nor does the average woman today want to be a fifties female. Consciousness, once raised, cannot be "lowered"; as Thomas Wolfe once said, "You can't go home again." Nonetheless, contemporary women do want something of the way it was; they wish to feel "soft" again, and they want to experience some corresponding strength from their men. In a fundamental way, this feeling is nothing more than a yearning to relax, to surrender into being a woman, a posture which requires less energy and less control. Yet such a surrender is too terrifying for the contemporary Amazon Woman, for she feels she has so much to *do* in the world.

In order to better understand the Amazon mode of thinking that permeates our culture, the next chapter will be devoted to a study of a great Amazon heroine of ancient Greek mythology.

CHAPTER TWO

Amazon Woman: Armed and Ready for Battle

The road down which the liberation movements of the last two decades have led us is a path to an Amazon society. Many contemporary women have taken the ideas of feminism and sexual equality and pushed them to an extreme, creating within themselves what might be viewed as an Amazon orientation to the world.

According to legend, the Amazon culture devalued men, eliminating them from all ruling positions, and, indeed, from practically all societal activities. In some versions of the Amazon legend, all the men were slaves. In others, "breeding males" from neighboring islands were used simply as a means of procreation, after which they were discarded in black widow spider fashion. In an alarmingly similar manner, many a modern Amazon Woman acquires and then discards her lovers. In the face of the great Amazon obsession with self-fulfillment and career, no man is that important.

In the original Amazon legend, Hippolyta, the Amazon queen, does ultimately form a relationship with a man, a relationship which leads to the fulfillment of her femininity but also to the ultimate downfall of the Amazon culture.

THE MYTH OF HIPPOLYTA

In *The Bull from the Sea,* Mary Renault's retelling of the Amazon tale, Theseus, king of Athens, accidentally comes upon the island of the Amazons and is astonished at what he sees.

"If these are the women," muses Theseus, "what are the men like?"[1] The women he sees are nothing like the soft domestic Athenian women he has known; they are warrior women—taut, athletic, swimming in the open sea, riding bareback upon their horses, armed for battle. Their bodies are gold from the sun, and their fair hair is drawn into long thick braids down their backs.

Theseus is struck instantly by Hippolyta, the Amazon queen. Never before has he seen a face of such flawless pride and beauty. He describes her as "like the moon goddess, deadly and innocent; gentle and fierce like the lion."[2] He wants her immediately, but soon realizes that there is no man of her tribe to fight for her. Indeed, he has met the warrior with whom he must do battle: Hippolyta herself.

How to go about fighting this battle is Theseus' next challenge, for he recognizes in Hippolyta a warrior of stature equal to his own. He senses that she will fight to the death, yet he wishes to take her alive. He has seen the woman behind the man, and he wants her for his own.

Before we continue this ancient tale, let us stop for a moment and consider its relevance to the contemporary Amazon Woman. Many women who read this charming little story can identify with the heroine

Hippolyta, Queen of the Amazons. They secretly long for a great "king" to come and sweep them off their tired feet. But most great men do not wish to do battle with women as did King Theseus; instead, they retreat from the fray and seek a gentler maiden. Nonetheless, it is only a fairy tale, so let us continue . . .

Consumed with passion, Theseus feels that his fate and indeed his very life are joined to that of the Amazon Queen. Cautiously, they encounter one another and, although their languages are different, they manage to communicate. Theseus states that he comes in peace, but Hippolyta is angered, for she knows that Theseus has witnessed an ancient ritual dance, "The Mystery," which is forbidden to the eyes of men. The penalty for this intrusion is death, and Hippolyta and the Moon Maidens of Artemis challenge Theseus and his men to battle. Theseus, however, says, "It was I who saw . . . I call you to single combat, King of the Maidens . . . Meet me, Hippolyta. A King cannot refuse a King."[3]

Hippolyta's sense of pride and honor is touched. She asks only that if she dies in combat, Theseus will spare her holy ritual ground and leave her Amazon maidens in peace. Theseus readily agrees to this and asks that, in the event of his death, he be buried on the mountain on which they both stand. Each agreeing to these terms, Theseus adds yet one more: "If I win, and you live, you shall take me for King and follow me." It is not here, however, that Hippolyta fully grasps his meaning, for she responds simply, "I fight to the death." The King, knowing that he will not kill her, replies, "Life and death are with the gods. Do you agree, then?"[4]

Against the wishes of her warrior women, Hippolyta consents, choosing as her weapons first javelins, then swords. She fights a fierce and deadly battle, so fierce and fast that the great King thinks to himself, "I am glad I have not this to do every day."[5] Finally, he makes a reckless lunge at her, throwing her to the ground. He holds her still for a very long time, trying to quiet her. Then he says, "The fight is over, Hippolyta. You are not dead. Will you keep your vow?"[6] She responds as if in a dream, "So be it." The great King of Athens then gathers her up in his arms and carries her off the field of battle, feeling their fates joined forever.

ALL FOR LOVE

Swept Away is the title of a Lina Wertmüller film that depicts a common female fantasy. Yet "swept away" is not what the contemporary Amazon Woman can afford to be, not if she values her career. Men can be swept away in love and continue to fare quite well in the business and political worlds, although a few empires have been known to crumble over a woman. The world stood by and watched in amazement as the Duke of Windsor abdicated his kingdom for "the woman I love." But the duke, I fear, was a great exception. Few men sacrifice all for love.

Women are different. In her insightful book *Knowing Woman*, Irene Claremont de Castillejo points out that even the strongest Amazon Woman, when in relationship with a man, will yield and adapt to him. It is second nature to women to put love first. We do it thoughtlessly, unintentionally, as a matter of course. The ideology of the past generation led us to believe that this was simply cultural conditioning, "nurture" as opposed to "nature," a way of behaving determined by men in a patriarchal society. But adaptation does indeed seem to come naturally to most women, especially in the presence of a man they truly love and admire. This has come to be a source of both embarrassment and concern for the Amazon woman of the nineteen-eighties, embarrassment for the weakness that she feels in "affairs of the heart" and concern for the potential invasion of her territory that such loss of control implies. For, like Hippolyta, most women who bond to a man will follow him. Territoriality is a strong male imperative. In love, it is almost always the woman who embraces the man's territory, not vice versa.

Hippolyta, like so many Amazon women of our time, knows only a life of self-sufficiency and independence. Bonding to a man is not part of her consciousness or expectation in life; in fact, it is forbidden by Amazon law. She is confused and upset by her surrender to this great King, but being a woman of honor, she follows him as promised. Shortly thereafter, in the dead of night, within the privacy of their tent, an Amazon Moon Maiden comes to her and slips her a dagger, the type used in the sacred ritual "Mystery" dance. Distraught and confused, Hippolyta approaches the sleeping Theseus, who is really awake but choosing to lie still and accept his fate. Instead of the thrust of a dagger, however, he feels instead the moist texture of her tears falling upon him, tears symbolic of her newfound feminine feelings. Fearing to shame her, he continues to lie still, but only for a moment, as Hippolyta turns quickly, preparing to thrust the dagger into her own heart instead.

With the swiftness he had learned in the Cretan bull ring, Theseus leaps from his bed, grabs Hippolyta's wrist, takes the dagger, and throws it into a corner of the tent. He attempts to comfort the unhappy Queen, saying, "One often stakes one's life on a little thing. So why not on a great one?" Hippolyta has no answer, for she still does not quite understand the significance of the path her life has so suddenly taken. She has, however, already begun to trust this King despite herself, and as the night rain falls from the sky, she falls into his strong arms and weeps.

"Love came to us as birth does," recalls Theseus, "knowing its own time better than those who wait for it. Though she knew less than any maid who had heard the women chatter, yet she knew more, knowing only me. My own life left me to live in her; with all women before I had been myself alone."[7]

Later, as she experiences a growing love and closeness with Theseus, Hippolyta confesses to him that her surrender on the battlefield left her feeling empty and negated. So divested of her Amazon armor was she that she thought to herself, "Now I am nothing."[8]

Most contemporary Amazon Women can identify with this, for they deeply fear the submersion of their own personalities in bonding to men. Bonding means attachment, and attachment requires some type of surrender and transformation of one's identity. But the Amazon Woman is often terrified that this transition might mean *losing* that identity, an identity which she has worked so long and so hard to create.

The myth of Hippolyta and Theseus, however, does not end with surrender or loss of identity. On the contrary, the tale goes on to weave a rich tapestry of Hippolyta's ensuing life in Athens and her psychological growth as a woman, a woman who learns to embrace a whole new identity. Contemporary Amazons need this too, but unfortunately, very few men, kingly or not, are willing to take the time or energy to get "the girl behind the boy" to surrender.

In war, of course, surrender means defeat. But in love (as Hippolyta discovers), surrender, for a woman, means victory. It involves embracing the totality of one's feminine potential, of opening oneself up to a man with complete trust and faith, not so much losing oneself as becoming more than one was before. But this is risky business, and one must be relaxed and open to it.

UPTIGHT AND STRESSED-OUT

The modern Amazon Woman is neither relaxed nor open. She is stressed and exhausted; her mind is working overtime. She is somehow always on the battlefield, not in a state of readiness, not receptive to a man. This, of course, is why so many contemporary women prefer the company of a "sensitive man," a man who can wind her down and play with her. Unfortunately, however, these men usually lack an aggressive edge and are often discarded for their lack of masculinity. Fairy tales are, in fact, just fairy tales, and Theseus is the stuff of which dreams are made, a fairy-tale king with enough sensitivity to take on a warrior woman. Most men would simply say, "Why bother?" Warrior women are too much trouble. Listen to W., a twenty-eight-year-old top executive:

"I have achieved tremendous power and success in the world. I'm strong and smart and very well respected. My mind is always working. And it doesn't just turn off when I'm in bed with a man. It keeps on focusing. My lover always complains about how long it takes to turn me on and wind me down. But frankly, working out a business deal in my head is usually a lot more exciting and compelling than having another orgasm."

For many contemporary women, sex means bondage instead of bonding. Many fantasize while having sex in order not to feel too close to their actual partners. Though there is nothing wrong with fantasy itself, which can often enhance a real sexual experience, fantasy can also be used as a distancing device, i.e., it seems safer imagining being with someone else, or even pretending to be someone else. To simply be oneself and surrender control to an actual man is far too threatening for many contemporary women.

And there are good reasons for these fears, for a woman who is truly in touch with her femininity surrenders only to a man she can trust and respect. The contemporary Amazon Woman intuitively knows this; if she surrenders at all, it is often at arm's length with men she is not always sure she even likes. Since bonding or loss of control feels devastating to her, she often chooses men she views as "beneath her station,'' men who may excite her for the moment but with whom she knows she shares no future.

Indeed, in a futureless relationship, true bonding is not only difficult, it is unwise. If a woman knows a relationship has no future, there is really no reason she should feel comfortable surrendering any part of her being, except perhaps her body, to a man. And even the physical aspects of male-female relationships have been touched by the contemporary woman's fear of dominance or control by a man.

ON TOP

For the extreme Amazon Woman, a sexual encounter can be an athletic event, a chance for her to show off the mastery of technique that makes her the star of her own private sexual Olympics. Since she is ''addicted to perfection,'' she feels she must be sexually perfect. That is, she must maintain control. This is a hard, extremely masculine point of view. She often has sex not for her own pleasure, but to assert her own sexual prowess by giving the man so much pleasure that he, in a sense, becomes her victim.

After a lecture on Amazon sexuality, C., an attractive advertising executive, explored her own powerful and perpetual desire to maintain control, even in the midst of sexual intercourse:

''I've done just about everything in bed, but my favorite position is being on top. On top, I feel triumphant, beautiful, in control of the action, not vulnerable and exposed as I sometimes feel in the 'missionary position.' I love the idea of having a big strong man lying there pleasurably helpless beneath me. A wounded man is a terrific turn-on. Once I had sex with a huge, muscular 'Wild Man from Samoa' (he actually lived there!) with his leg in a cast. He was a very lusty man, but all he could do was get hard and lie on his back—this was fine with me, since it is one of the few ways I can come.

"But coming is not really my goal in sex. I really just want to be desired above all women by the men I am with. I am careful to uncover the sexual needs and desires of each of my men, what kinds of postures and behaviors I must assume so that each will declare me 'the best.' I consider the liaison complete when word gets back to me, as it invariably does, that I am indeed 'great in bed.' This usually takes about three months. At that point, after I know I've 'won,' I usually leave the man, moving on to conquer another."

This type of woman is always competing, always working, even when she appears to be doing nothing. She is so performance-oriented, even in bed, that she is in a perpetual state of tension and exhaustion. A true warrior, she is constantly armed and ready for battle. She is interested in being best and being free, not in bonding to a man for life.

But what really is the value of bonding and attachment for the contemporary woman (other than her obvious need for procreation)? Given her typically poor choice of sexual partners, actual bonding for the Amazon would indeed be foolhardy. Unlike her mother and grandmother, she chooses men who are not "husband material," but rather those who pleasure her senses, or perhaps her intellect, for the moment. Her powers of discrimination seem flawed; she doesn't seem to know what a "good man" really is. If one is going to bond or surrender, it only makes sense that it be with a friend, not a stranger, with a lifetime partner, not a one-night stand.

Actually, men also fail to use their discriminating powers in love, yet it isn't as devastating to them as it is to women. Indeed, it is not devastating at all; it can be a boost to the male ego to visit a house of prostitution, to make it with the "fast girl" on campus, to score with the easy lay. There is a very primitive desire on the part of men to mate downward, as there is an equally primitive desire on the part of women to mate upward. I believe this instinct is rooted in gender biology: Men physically go "downward"; that is, they penetrate women. Moreover, it has to do with a man's biological need for dominance and control. A man does not want to be around that which he cannot control; it feels castrating to him. Developmentally, his psychological mission in life is to separate from his mother, not to be dominated by a woman any longer. So to pick a dominant and strong woman whom he can't control—a woman who negotiates for more power, money, and advantage in the world, who is always asserting her will and her opinions—is dangerous for him because it subliminally presents the risk of castration. And this, of course, is psychological annihilation of his manhood, certain death.

Both men and women are born of woman. But a man needs to differentiate himself from his mother much more strongly than a woman does. A man starts out his life controlled by a woman, his mother; his leap into manhood requires that he break with his mother and exert his own control in the world. This is known as "autonomy" and is central to the development of the male ego. Woman is born of woman

too, but there is less need for a woman to differentiate herself from her mother, as they are both of the
same sex. Irene Claremont de Castillejo points out in
her book *Knowing Woman* that a woman's connection to her mother, and indeed to ''Mother Earth,'' is
central to her being. She quotes one independent
young professional woman as stating:

''You can't think what a relief it is to know I do
not need to break with my mother, to know that it is
through her that I am a link in a chain back into the
past and forward into the future.''[9]

A man, however, *must* differentiate himself from
his mother, as he is not a woman; he is a man. The
extent to which a man does this (and his mother
allows him to do it) varies greatly from man to man,
and some men succeed in this regard more than
others. But because all men must strive for this separation in their psychological development, it often
appears as if men are struggling for superiority or
dominance over women. This struggle is, in fact,
nothing more than a manifestation of man's great
need to be free, individuated from woman, in control
of his own destiny.

The mature male is a natural protector. He enjoys
and exercises his strength and his power, both of
which validate his freedom and his developmental
differences from women. But such men do not like to
war with women, at least not for very long. Mature
men, whom I will henceforth refer to as ''Actual
Men,'' like to embrace a woman for her uniquely
feminine attributes, which continue to enhance his
ever-developing manhood and differentiate him as
man.

Some highly accomplished and intellectually evolved

women do indeed have satisfying personal relationships with mature men. But these are special women who are in touch with their feminine aspects, and therefore relate to men in a noncompetitive manner. Such women truly enjoy men, take strength and refuge in them, and delight in the special feelings which men arouse. A feminine *attitude* toward men has nothing to do with a woman's place in the world, but this is poorly understood by most contemporary women. Women today, even those of meager accomplishment, have a competitive attitude toward the opposite sex, struggling with them to be "better men than they are."

The Amazon Woman fails to understand the psychological and developmental differences between the sexes. She insists on battling. She needs to be best in everything: in work, in conversation, in relationship, and in love. It is difficult for her to be feminine and supportive with men—especially strong men—because competitiveness is at the heart of her psyche and sexuality.

Take the case of J., a thirty-year-old sales representative. J. was under the illusion that she was "winning" in her competitive relationship with her boyfriend of three years. She never allowed him to enter much of her life or "conquer" her territory. In retrospect, she realizes that she wound up with a Pyrrhic victory; that is, she thought she had won, but in fact she had lost. No real bonding had occurred, for she had never allowed this man to get really close to her. "One of the reasons that I stayed three years with him," she says, "was that I enjoyed feeling superior to him. I liked being always 'one up' on him."

P., a voluptuous, sexually active thirty-six-year-old attorney, is as competitive in love as she is in the courtroom. "Most of the men I go out with just can't keep up with me; I don't even take them seriously," says P. "But every now and then I meet a really terrific man, someone who's got it all together, a guy who not only keeps up with me but far surpasses me. And it's great for a while. He's struck by my beauty and charm, just like in the fairy tales. We find each other stimulating and exciting. But then, after just a few weeks or even days, I can't seem to resist being difficult. I suppose it's their power and mastery that gets my competitive edge going. The ensuing competition takes many forms. I may argue with them over silly things or break dates to prove I'm busier than they are. I'll find ways to demonstrate my financial self-sufficiency, like picking up the check at dinner. When it comes to sex with powerful men like this, I can get quite perverse. I let them know that I'm in control, that I may do outrageous sexual things, but they can't *make* me do anything. Then, after a while, they stop trying to make me do anything. They just drop me."

The response of a modern-day Theseus to an armored Amazon[10] like P. is simply to leave the field of battle. He fights long and hard enough all day in the business world; why should he want to put up with it at home? He flees from such a woman, not because he is "threatened," as many Amazon Women claim, but because he knows better. An Actual Man knows what he wants, and he goes after it. Carl Jung, in fact, defined masculinity as "knowing what one wants and doing what is necessary to achieve it."[11]

If he doesn't get what he wants, he goes elsewhere. It is more than just a power play; it is a question of his sense of manhood. To simply give up a bit of power in a fair negotiation is not difficult for a mature male. It is his *manhood* with which he does not wish to part. If all this translates into the cliché of the "frail male ego," so be it. It is the way of the world, and of life itself.

The mature woman's ego strength, her sense of herself, is indeed *stronger* than a man's, as she need not differentiate herself as woman; she simply *is*. She is a woman, born of woman, not needing to prove anything. What I find the modern woman often fails to see is that despite her accomplishments, she still has a unique role to play as mediator to man, a role which she may choose for herself or not, depending on her personality, her needs, and her goals. It has been my strong impression that the contemporary woman does desire loving connections with men, but simply does not know how to establish them. The modern woman's new consciousness has severely tilted her personality in such a way that she is out of touch with her feminine reality and can relate only "man to man," for, in all her interactions, she is leading with her male or Amazon aspect.

POSSESSED BY THE DEVIL

Carl Jung called this Amazon aspect of female personality the "animus," the male part of the woman. Many contemporary women may object to this conceptualization, but it has long been acknowledged in cultures all over the world that within every woman is a man, and within every man there is a woman.

This is to say that we all have male and female aspects to our personalities. By male and female, we refer not to gender, but to modes of existence and ways of being. In certain cultures, in fact, these terms don't refer specifically to human gender, but to concepts and images. The Oriental symbol of "yin and yang" illustrates this point. "Yin" is feminine, but also means dark, earth, water, moon, the south side of the mountain, feeling, and intuition. "Yang" is masculine, but it also means light, sky, air, sun, the north side of the mountain, logic, and rational thought. The yin-yang symbol is dark and light, both masculine and feminine, a symbol of the continuity of life itself.

We are, in fact, all both male and female. But men are still primarily male, and women are still primarily female. In the past, it could certainly be said that the male part of the female personality was but a small part of her total functioning. This, however, is no longer true, for the contemporary woman tends to be "animus-possessed"; i.e., in the grip of her masculine consciousness. She vaguely suspects that there may be other parts of herself that lie dormant, but she does not know how to get to them. Seized by her power drives, longing for bonding but terrified of it, she often feels in the grip of the devil himself.

"I feel as if I've been driving a train that's going a hundred miles an hour for thirty years," says one workaholic Amazon Woman. "If I try to stop and just *be* instead of do, do, *do*, I'm afraid that the train will go careening off the tracks and my whole life will explode in a terrible fire."

It is difficult to communicate on paper the true difference in a psychological sense between being and doing. M. Esther Harding, in *The Way of All Women*, characterizes the quintessential feminine woman as psychologically "pre-conscious."[12] She operates in a natural, intuitive fashion, utilizing her feelings as opposed to her intellect. She doesn't think analytically or strategically about what she does at all. She just *is*.

Turning her head off in order to feel her feelings poses a serious problem for the contemporary Amazon woman, who needs to be perpetually on guard. Like Hippolyta, she often lives in a world without men, with no one to defend her. She has to fight her own battles, stand up for herself. This defensive posture in life does not lend itself well to receptive femininity nor to the feelings which accompany it. "Out of control" is what today's woman cannot afford to be. Indeed, she cannot afford to just *be* at all.

When a musician friend of mine told me that he was going back on tour, I declared that it must be wonderful to "feel productive again," to which he responded, "I feel productive just being alive." I, on the other hand, did not feel productive just being alive. I needed to do something in order to feel productive and valuable. In those days, I needed to be *doing*, not simply being, in order to feel alive at all.

Hippolyta, shortly after she surrendered in battle to Theseus, said, "I am nothing." To an Amazon, just "being" is being nothing; it is equated in her mind with the entire disintegration of the personality and a sense of profound failure. The less she does, in her mind, the less she is worth.

Doing, with a morbid fear of just being, is compulsive behavior. Contemporary women in general are highly obsessive-compulsive; they have to be—to get their work done. Compulsive behavior is indeed highly efficient since it is so focused and intense. Yet a compulsive attitude greatly narrows the range of a woman's existence and cuts her off from her feminine feelings.

Beneath the surface of the overstriven Superwoman is often a frightened little girl, fearful of losing control, of falling apart, of simply being. Feminism, having promised her a stronger sense of her own identity, has given her little more than an identity *crisis*. Unlike the fortunate Amazon Queen Hippolyta, there is no King Theseus who is willing to do battle with her and help resolve that crisis. For the most part, the Amazon Woman is once again challenged to go it alone and discover her lost femininity by herself.

In *Modern Women in Europe*, Jung said that man's consciousness could not proceed further until women's consciousness caught up with him. And over the last two decades, this is exactly what women have been doing. Women are now, like men, oriented toward doing, not being. In terms of the psyche, "doing" is characterized by a *focused* consciousness; "being" by a *diffuse* awareness. We are all familiar with the feminist term "consciousness-raising." For me, this term really means "consciousness-*changing*," for the feminist and sexual revolutions changed female consciousness from that of diffuse awareness (being) to the more masculine mode of focused consciousness (doing).

I cannot help but wonder if Dr. Jung, a great visionary, would have been surprised and perhaps disappointed at the results of the highly developed

focused consciousness of many Amazon Women today. Jung expected that this newfound male attitude—
the development of the woman's animus-Amazon
aspect—would be utilized in the service of her
femininity. But the opposite, in fact, has happened.
This newfound power has been utilized by women,
albeit unconsciously, to *separate* themselves from
their feminine aspects—aspects which will be explored in the following chapter.

CHAPTER THREE

The Four Aspects of Woman: Amazon, Mother, Madonna, Courtesan

Bonding is one of our most basic human drives. We are first bonded to our mothers; these bonds shift and change and are reestablished with other people, new partners, and children. It is universally acknowledged, even by the most naive, that we start to die from the moment that we are born and that it is a terrible thing to die alone. Bonding eases that terror. Indeed, bonding is the central issue of living, yet the feminist and sexual revolutions encouraged women to "break the bonds."

John Donne said that "no man is an island." The contemporary woman is experiencing the consequences of overstriven self-sufficiency (Big Lie Number Nine). No one can argue with a woman's right to seek employment and become economically self-sufficient. But what no one anticipated were the emotional consequences that followed these behaviors. Self-sufficiency in women has its roots in two sources: (1) rugged nineteen-sixties individualism, and (2) the feminist movement, both of which encouraged women to find themselves *before* they bonded, the erroneous belief being that if one did that, one would be a better partner. In fact, the opposite is often true; the more independent one becomes, the less one is usually willing to compromise that independence. This is commonly known as being set in one's ways.

Bonding is not an intellectual experience. It is emotional, spiritual, and sexual. Women who have been living only by their intellect are women who are aging without bonding, and they are trying to ignore this fact as though it had no relevance to the whole of their lives. Much of my time on the radio these days is spent in teaching women how to bond again, how to live and feel *as women*.

Several years ago, I did not know myself. It is said that we only teach that which we have to learn, and I had a strong yearning to melt my Amazon armor and get on with the feminine side of my life. In my research, I stumbled across a four-page paper by a fascinating Zurich analyst named Toni Wolff who studied under Jung and subsequently became his mistress. The paper, entitled ''Structural Forms of the Feminine Psyche,''[1] intrigued me. In her lengthy analyses of hundreds of women, Miss Wolff identified four basic archetypes of woman, ''archetypes'' being universal ways of thinking about things, usually represented as images in the unconscious mind. Wolff called these four archetypal aspects the Amazon Woman, the Mother, the Medial Woman, and the Hetaira. The Amazon was identified with her intellect, the Mother with her nurturing capabilities, the Medial type with her inspirational abilities, and the Hetaira with her personal relationship to man. I could find nothing else written on this subject and decided to evolve my own theoretical construct based on the early work of Miss Wolff, broadening and developing it in such a way as to shed light on the psychological dilemma of the contemporary woman.

In my formulation, I am continuing to call the Amazon aspect the Amazon and the Mother aspect the Mother, as both these terms have great clarity. The Amazon Woman is highly focused, ambitious, assertive, goal-oriented, and self-sufficient. She relates to the men in her life as companions, co-workers, and competitors.

The Mother is a caretaker, a woman who thrives upon her attachments to others. She nurtures not only her own children, but other relatives and female friends, as well as the men in her life.

What Miss Wolff refers to as the Medial aspect of woman, I will refer to as the Madonna: the aspect of woman which is inspirational in nature and imparts standards, values, and ideals. The Madonna is reflective. She embodies the quintessentially feminine virtues of patience, silence, and faith, that part of woman that is closest to nature and to her own soul. Men enjoy her because she is so reflective of their own moods and feelings. This type of woman does not seek to attain greatness for herself; rather, she inspires the man in her life to greatness, supporting him unconditionally in *his* quest for fulfillment and achievement.

I have renamed the Hetaira aspect the Courtesan. Geisha, playmate, and whore are other terms for this aspect, but none of these words quite communicates the full meaning of the Greek term Hetaira, a woman who operates primarily *in personal relationship to man* on intellectual and emotional as well as sexual levels. "Courtesan" comes closest; the other words— "geisha," "playmate," and especially "whore"—

imply a position in life somehow subservient to man. The Courtesan does indeed sing a kind of harmony to her man, but she is not subservient to him in any way. Nor is she looked down upon for her role. Indeed, the Courtesan is an aspect of woman which men have adored and appreciated down through the ages. Such women have often been exalted to positions of great power in the lives of these men.

It is my belief that all four aspects of a woman's psyche (Amazon, Mother, Madonna, Courtesan) should ultimately be experienced and incorporated into a woman's personality over the course of her lifetime. Most theories of personality, both old and new, deal with integration of the personality, a sense of wholeness and completion among many different parts. And this theory is no exception. It takes a long time, of course, to become all that we might be, and each woman must look within herself to discover what aspects of her personality are yet in need of developing.

In her original formulation, Toni Wolff speculated that women of an earlier time were perhaps characterized by only one aspect of personality, the aspect which was most consistent with her nature. Over time, however, female personality evolved in such a way that it came to be dominated by *two* aspects, the other two tending to stay in the background. As such, there are six different possible types of pairings: Amazon-Courtesan, Amazon-Mother, Amazon-Madonna, Mother-Madonna, Madonna-Courtesan, and Mother-Courtesan. Each of these types of women is easily recognizable, as the following examples will illustrate.

AMAZON-COURTESAN

A career woman with a playful or sexual aspect to her personality would be an Amazon-Courtesan type with her Mother-Madonna in the background. Helen Gurley Brown projects an excellent example of this type. Her strong Amazon drive has rendered her the author of two best-selling books and the publisher of one of the most popular women's magazines in the world. The sexual nature of her writings hints at her Courtesan aspect, which is also apparent in her devoted relationship with her husband, a man who is at least her equal in professional success and power. Ms. Brown has no children, nor is she well known for advocating moral virtue; as such, her Mother and Madonna aspects take a back seat to her dynamic and highly provocative personality.

Zsa Zsa Gabor seems to be another example of an Amazon-Courtesan type. Her Amazon ambitions have brought her great success as an actress/personality. Ms. Gabor's Courtesan aspect is apparent in her playful relations with powerful men. She rides horses and plays golf well enough, though not with any athletic seriousness. When a friend of mine asked her why she acquired these skills, she replied, ''I was raised to be a companion to man.'' Such is the operative mode of the Courtesan: She plays games her man likes to play, not to win but simply to accompany him.

AMAZON-MOTHER

An Amazon-Mother is achievement-oriented, yet defines herself in relation to others, to her family, her friends, her following. Erma Bombeck seems to be the quintessential Amazon-Mother. Highly accomplished as a journalist, she bases much of her writing on her amusing experiences as a mother. Many female politicians, such as Golda Meir and Indira Gandhi, could be considered Amazon-Mothers. Driven by their Amazon aspects to achieve personal fame and power, they are equally motivated by a love for their "people" that closely resembles unconditional maternal devotion.

AMAZON-MADONNA

Amazon-Madonnas combine high ideals with strong personal drives. Gloria Steinem, writer, publisher, and feminist theorist, and Dr. Joyce Brothers, popular media psychologist, seem to be two extremely different women. Yet both are Amazon-Madonna types, each in her own way exemplifying feminine virtue as well as accomplishment. Joan of Arc is perhaps the best-known Amazon-Madonna in history. Guided by the "voices" of her soul, she donned the proverbial Amazon armor to lead the armies of France to victory.

These first three, the Amazon types, are far easier to identify than the other three pairings; a woman with a strong Amazon aspect often projects herself externally, focusing upon making herself and her deeds known to the world. We know who she is *because* she is an Amazon. The Mother-Madonna, Madonna-Courtesan, and Mother-Courtesan types are not so "high-profile." Thus, it is more difficult to come up with prominent examples of these types, for these women by definition are not women of prominence—except, that is, in their private universe, where they may well reign supreme.

MOTHER-MADONNA

The Mother-Madonna rarely achieves fame, unless it is through her husband and children, especially her sons but sometimes her daughters. She is the type of woman who mothers everyone—her children, her children's friends, her husband, her relatives, even strangers—if they let her. She has high standards and a strong sense of right and wrong. She likes to give advice, sometimes gentle, oftentimes harsh. She never dresses provocatively but is always well groomed. She "ages well." Patience and a curious sense of serenity are characteristic of the Mother-Madonna. She is the quintessential "good woman"; Chaucer's "dutiful wife" whose "value is above gold" was such a woman. Rose Kennedy also is an example of a Mother-Madonna, an inspirational woman of faith, patience, and devotion whose men became legendary American heroes. Of course, if it was not for the greatness of these men in her life whom she inspired, she would not be known to us at all.

MADONNA-COURTESAN

The Madonna-Courtesan woman has perhaps been best epitomized on film. She is the *femme fatale,* the "mystery woman" about whom men fantasize and create great works of art and poetry. She is the ultimate *femme inspiratrice*. Greta Garbo and Jean Harlow were actresses of the Madonna-Courtesan type; these women were worshipped, not just lusted after. The Courtesan aspect in each of them exuded a highly sensual allure; the Madonna centered them spiritually. Perhaps what is so attractive about the Madonna-

Courtesan is that she combines the feminine polarities of fire and ice. Many men may desire the Madonna-Courtesan sexually, but few actually get to enjoy her; she is a discriminating woman. Notice that it is the addition of the Madonna aspect to the Courtesan which makes the sexy woman classy.

MOTHER-COURTESAN

While the Madonna-Courtesan is "fire and ice," the Mother-Courtesan is all fire, all warmth of spirit, all heated passion. At its best, her warmth glows, attracts, and nurtures. At its worst, her fire is so high that it consumes; thus we have the overprotective mother and oversolicitous wife who smothers those she loves. The Mother-Courtesan is defined totally by her relationship to others, to friends, to children, to animals, and certainly always to men. She is a great giver. Young Mother-Courtesans are usually the first girls to have boyfriends. These are the girls who are easy to be with; often they are just "easy," period. Lacking the discriminating standards of the Madonna and the goal-oriented focus of the Amazon, the Mother-Courtesan is easily had and often used. Since she defines herself in terms of relationship, she is often a "victim" of circumstances. At worst, she is psychologically and physically abused by others. At best, she is revered as a great mother and wife, cherished and loved in a way that Madonnas—too cold and pure for lavish demonstrations of affection—often are not. Of all the types described, the Mother-Courtesan is the most affectionate, appealing, and almost totally nonthreatening. Love is the most important aspect of this woman's life. Often, however, she lacks a strong spiritual center, because her sense of self is so ill defined. Such a woman usually hits a crisis point in her life when she must find that sense of herself independently of others.

Marilyn Monroe is a well-known example of a Mother-Courtesan type. Although not an actual mother (it is important to note here that the Mother aspect of personality need not have anything to do with actual maternity), she was extremely "motherly" to all who knew her and a great companion to men. Monroe was loved by the American public in a personal, passionate way that Garbo and Harlow were not. Her warmth conveyed unconditional love and easy acceptance. Unfortunately, like so many Mother-Courtesan types, Monroe, a great giver of herself, never truly received in kind; she never got as good as she gave.

It is my conviction that over a lifetime, the integrated woman must assimilate all of these aspects of her womanhood into her personality to experience herself as a complete person.

Women in earlier decades generally started off life as Mother-Madonnas, possibly developing their Amazon-Courtesan aspects later. Freed from their fear of pregnancy, they became more sexual and aggressive in the world. Contemporary women have been doing just the opposite. As sexy, accomplished women, they usually develop their Amazon-Courtesan aspects first. As they reach their early to mid-thirties, however, they start to experience a kind of emptiness and begin to yearn for enduring connections with men and children. A creeping sense of uneasiness starts to pervade their consciousness, especially in the case of the woman who has been strongly led by her masculine drives for many years.

At this stage in development, some women "take the bull by the horns" and utilize their masculine Amazon energies in the interest of their femininity. One such Amazon Woman, a thirty-one-year-old beautiful blond publicity director of an international publishing company, made such a decision in the interest of the fulfillment of her Mother-Madonna aspect. She selected as her mate an appropriate man in his mid-forties, and on their second evening together announced to him that if they were to become involved seriously, she desired children. She realized that the relationship might come to nothing but a pleasant affair, but in the event that something was to come of it, she simply wished to inquire as to whether he would be open to the possibility of starting a new family. This is an excellent example of Amazon aggression in the interests of one's femininity and, in this case, it worked. The gentleman in question was amenable to children, and he and my friend have plans for marriage.

TICK-TOCK

Many Amazon Women, however, do not make this transition as easily or successfully, finding it prohibitively difficult to change or to find an appropriate male partner with whom they might exercise these new roles and attitudes. Thus we come to the dilemma of many a contemporary Amazon Woman: the merciless ticking away of the biological clock, limiting her opportunities for the literal expression of motherhood, coupled with her reduced chances for marriage as she ages. If the Amazon-Courtesan wishes to become a Mother-Madonna, at least in relation to men, her chances are pretty slim over the age of thirty-five. Options exist, of course, for exercising these dimensions of personality in other ways. One need not mother actual children; one may express one's nurturing capabilities in a wide variety of ways. Similarly, the expression of the Madonna, which Wolff called the Medial aspect, need not be exercised only in relation to men. This aspect can be developed through devotion to any cause or ideal. Still, this is not the road which most women truly wish to take. Few of us are Joan of Arc or even Gloria Steinem. Most women seek the fulfillment of their Mother-Madonna aspects through union with a man and fulfillment of their biology through maternity.

In *Reality Therapy,* Dr. William Glasser points out that the denial of reality is a hallmark of neurosis.[2] If this be the case, it would appear that the average contemporary woman is severely neurotic in her denial of her biological clock and the reality of aging. Once again, we return to the fact that the contemporary woman has been deluded by the "Big Lies of Liberation," which suggest that her life is rich and full because she has professional and sexual stimulation. Indeed, as she fills herself with these substitutes for genuine enduring devotion and love, she doesn't allow herself to feel her profound emptiness until she is somehow confronted by the reality of her life, then forced to deal with her lack of fulfillment as a woman.

SHUT OFF FROM AIR

Such is the case for Sylvia Plath's protagonist in her novel *The Bell Jar.*[3] Esther Greenwood is an Amazon Woman cut off from her feelings and feminine instincts. She frequently suffers from profound depression and existential despair since her identification with work and power and the world of the intellect is not sufficient to fulfill her deepest longings. Esther is a straight-A student, living ironically in a hotel called "The Amazon." Underlying Esther's accomplishments is a deep-seated depression and sense of emptiness in her life. She makes no real emotional connections with her lovers and, in typical Amazon fashion, finds various mechanisms with which to detach herself. One such mechanism, for example, is collecting "men with interesting names." In similar fashion, the Amazon Woman of today may collect men who are "exciting" in a wide variety of ways or select them merely on the basis of their usefulness in a given situation, i.e., he looks good in a tuxedo, he has drugs, he has professional connections, he's good in bed, etc. Finally, Esther starts to experience her life as being lived in a "bell jar," shut off from air, life, and feeling, and starts having suicidal fantasies. Esther's redemption is found in the discovery and redemption of the feminine within herself. With the help of an understanding and compassionate therapist, she is able to contact the deeper feelings inside of her, her womanhood. Put most simply, she is able to accept herself just for *being* and not for *doing*.

Such is the dilemma of the contemporary Amazon Woman who feels valued only for *doing*, that is, for her accomplishments and achievements, and not for her *being*, her quintessential feminine qualities. Like Hippolyta in the Amazon myth, the woman who is divested of her position in life often falls into serious despair and suicidal depression. In fact, in *The Bell*

Jar, Esther does not become suicidal until she has to move out of the big city and back to her small hometown, where for the first time in her adult life she has nothing to do but to face herself. Remember Hippolyta who, when conquered by Theseus, thought, "Now I am nothing." She was, in fact, far from nothing. What she was experiencing was her extreme vulnerability and receptivity, probably for the first time in her life. It is frightening for the Amazon Woman to experience this deep, vulnerable part of herself, to recognize that there is nothing she need "do," that she can find real strength in simply "being."

It is my impression that the contemporary woman is severely tilted toward the Amazon or masculine aspect of her personality; that is, oriented toward power as opposed to love. Often she excludes her Mother, Madonna, and Courtesan aspects, which are feminine in nature. She either postpones motherhood or gives it very short shrift; is not in touch with her Madonna (too old-fashioned), and uses her Courtesan, if at all, only in the service of sexual pleasure. The contemporary Amazon Woman is goal-directed, her energies utilized in the external world, not in the creation of loving relationships or connections.

"THE LITTLE WOMAN"

It should be pointed out here that women who are in touch with their femininity are not necessarily lacking in the Amazon aspect. That is, they are not necessarily thoughtless nondirected creatures. We are all familiar with the image of the "dumb blonde," whom everyone secretly suspects is not so dumb. I'm

reminded of the dinner party I attended with a bois-
terous, obnoxious, very wealthy man who kept ignor-
ing his French wife mutely seated at the table— and
referring to her as "The Little Woman." Finally, in
frustration, I asked, "Does she speak?" and she
replied, "Oh, yes. I may be silent. But I'm not dumb."
Such a woman can have enormous power. In a woman
such as this the Amazon potential—her intelligence,
her drive, her forcefulness, her focused consciousness
—is used in the service of her femininity. And this
power has been greatly underestimated by women in
contemporary America.

Conversely, some women are estranged from their
masculine aspects, and such women are pathologically passive. These women do not use their Amazon
at all, neither in the service of their effectiveness in
the marketplace nor in the service of their femininity.
This, too, presents a serious problem, for a woman
must be in touch with her masculine principle in
order to properly direct her life and be a balanced and
dignified person. Similarly, the man who is cut off
from his feminine aspect, the man who totally denies
his feelings, his sensitivity, his receptivity, is also
pathologically disturbed; that is, he is a caricature of
a man.

For both men and women, integrating the different
aspects of a personality into a harmonious whole has
always been a lifetime challenge. It is my feeling,
however, that the contemporary woman has a unique
problem. When Toni Wolff wrote her paper on the
four aspects of womanhood, she said that women of
earlier times led with only one aspect of personality.
In her own time, she felt that women operated under
two aspects. And I would say that at this point, the

contemporary woman, with all she is doing and trying to be, is operating under *three* aspects of feminine personality. And if she looks closely to see the aspect in which she is inferior, she will probably find it to be her Madonna. The emptiness which she experiences, manifested through a wide range of behavior disorders—sexual promiscuity, food and drug addictions, stress reactions, and obsessive-compulsive behaviors of all kinds—is due to what I call the "Crisis in the Madonna," and it is to this issue that the next chapter will be addressed.

CHAPTER FOUR

Crisis in the Madonna:
No Longer a Lady

One night at Vassar College, near midnight, a convocation was called in the chapel by Miss Sarah Gibson Blanding, dean of students. We marched quietly out of our dormitories, mystified by this unexpected event. Miss Blanding, an elegant white-haired matriarch from the deep South, looked pained. She took the stage with her usual regal composure, but her voice was shaking and filled with tears. It had come to her attention, she began, that a large number of women, Vassar girls, had been spending their nights in various motel rooms in the Poughkeepsie environs for the purposes of sexual liaison. To think, she went on, that women of "our caliber" would "want such a thing" for ourselves was unbelievable to her. Vassar women had always been leaders, their high standards of intellect matched only by their equally high standards of ethics and morality. What had happened to us all? Where did we think we were going with this thoughtless behavior?

Where, indeed? It was the 1960s. Miss Blanding's chastity lecture made international headlines throughout the week; the corridors of MAIN (the student union) were papered with reports on "The Vassar Sex Scandal" in several different languages. I was twenty, still a virgin, clinging tenaciously to a morality that was rapidly becoming passé. I married shortly thereafter, divorced fourteen years later, joined the sexual revolution, and played a fast game of catch-up with a new set of rules. Today, twenty years later, I can answer Miss Blanding's question as to where we were going, for now we are there.

The contemporary American woman is undergoing what I view as a crisis in the Madonna. What was once valued by her, by society, and by men seems not to be valued any longer. Today's woman scores no points for chastity before marriage; a woman over twenty-five who is still a virgin is thought to be very odd indeed. Nobody is quite certain what a "lady" is anymore, and furthermore, nobody really seems to care. On the contrary, to be a lady can be an impediment for a woman in contemporary society, for to be a lady is a very different thing than to be a gentleman. To be a gentleman is to be honorable, to play by the rules. To be a lady is to be ever gentle, soft, gracious, attending to the little niceties that make the world a more comfortable and civilized place in which to live. These attributes are of little value to the contemporary Amazon Woman, as they markedly slow down her efficiency in the working world. The soft woman is a pushover, easy prey, and the last generation of women has made a concerted effort to "toughen up."[1]

Not all old-fashioned values have gone out of vogue, however. Virginity is quite passé, but it appears that fidelity during marriage is still expected. This is often rather difficult for today's woman, who has experienced a wide range of lovers and is often extremely bored within the confines of marital sex. Never before in history have so many women aban-

doned their husbands, good husbands, hu..
only sin against them was their stability.

It used to be that women were looking fu
ity, peace, and continuity in their lives. They
profound sense of the future. But many a contemporary woman lives by the Gestalt credo of the "here
and now." This actually cuts her off from her true
feelings, her connections to the past and the future.
Both dissociations are equally serious. If you cut
people off from their past, you take away not only
their joyful memories but also normal human emotions like shame, guilt, and regret. "He who fails to
learn from the past is doomed to repeat it" makes
psychological as well as historical sense. We must
stay attached to our past in order to learn. We must
stay in touch with the future in order to have faith
and hope. "Here and now" philosophies rob us of
these essential human qualities and separate us from
the Madonna aspect of our feminine psyche.

THE GREAT DIVORCE WAVE

In the last decade of our history, the contemporary
American woman has sought adventure, self-gratification, and sexual excitement. Her faith, her hope,
and her dreams were invested in herself and her
future; she showed little faith in men and marriage
for providing her fulfillment in life. Indeed, the Amazon Women who left their husbands in the great
divorce wave of the last decade did not know the
meaning of the song "Stand by Your Man." Over
the years, I've heard dozens of explanations as to
"why" they left, and the reasons vary greatly. Each
divorced a different kind of husband for a different

.ype of reason. But what all these women had in common was their lack of *faith;* i.e., the belief that with their feminine help and support, they and their men could pull through their relationship and life difficulties successfully. This was the old-time way of the Madonna, the way it was, the way that has inspired great cultures for centuries.

It was the Madonna part of a woman whose faith triumphed above all, who took a man for richer or for poorer, in sickness and in health. But many women of the last generation have abdicated the Madonna aspect of their personalities, retiring it to the dark recesses of their unconscious, like a useless antique. Faith, patience, and devotion became relics of an earlier time, of little use to a self-involved, power-driven woman. At the first sign of their husbands' imperfections or weaknesses, they deserted them; the role of *femme inspiratrice* or "muse to man" was no longer in vogue. Women wanted to be free of men sexually and economically. Married or unmarried, the American woman took a flying leap down from the pedestal only to discover, a decade later, a crying need for reunion with her almost forgotten Madonna aspect.

Following a lecture, "The Four Aspects of Woman," K., age forty, a highly accomplished Amazon Woman, documented in detail her flight from her marriage and from traditional values:

"Shortly before my marriage ended, when I was in my early thirties, I went to a prestigious black-tie dinner in Boston where men from all walks of life were honored for their outstanding accomplishments. I was asked to serve on the board of governors of this organization. I decked myself out in a flowing, form-

fitting, strapless gown of white jersey with a match-
ing cape and hood, and I swept into the grand ballroom
where the first man I laid eyes on was not one of
these successful, distinguished businessmen, but the
half-breed Indian driver for a Texas entrepreneur. He
was twenty-eight years old, a cross between Burt
Reynolds and Marlon Brando. At the end of the
dinner, I saw him leave. I gave him five minutes to
get just a little bit ahead of me. Then I left the
ballroom, and quite slowly began the march to my
bedroom door. As I turned the corner and started up
the stairs, I saw him sitting there at the top of the
stairs. He was out of his full uniform, in a Stanley
Kowalski tight T-shirt rolled up at the sleeves and
tight, tight jeans. We said not one word to each
other. We walked into my room, closed the door,
and from that moment, which was about midnight,
until six o'clock in the morning, we made love. I had
my period, which fazed him not at all. He said,
'Indians worship menstrual blood; it is sterile and
sacred.' He was the most sexual man I have ever
met. I've never forgotten him.

"About three months later, he came to New York.
I went to the hotel where he was staying and went to
bed with him one more time. It was not nearly as
exciting as our first time, and certainly much briefer.
I realized that I never wanted to see him again, and
never did.

"The thing that I felt most strongly following this
adventure was the complete abandonment of the
Madonna aspect of my personality, which I had come
to view as almost a burden. I was tired of being a
'good girl' and I longed for adventure. Here, in one
night, I had broken all the rules. I had gone to bed

with a total stranger, a man far beneath my station in life, wordlessly, shamelessly, and during my period. I felt wild and victorious, oddly free, disconnected, unattached to the past. It was all part of being 'independent,' my own woman. From then on, I was as driving and compulsive in my sexual adventures as I was in my professional life; the power drive seemed to cut into both realms. Sex became associated with power, not with love, although I don't believe I realized that at the time.

"The compulsion to experiment sexually continued for the next several years, after which I grew weary and began to long for a reunion with the Madonna aspect of my personality. Suddenly, I wanted sex to mean something; I wanted it to be connected to values and to love. At first, it was hard for me to view my body as special and to seek a spiritual as well as physical union with a man. Yet, as I 'tried on' my newfound chastity, I was astonished to discover the feelings of the very young, shy, Madonna-like girl I used to be, and in many respects still was."

This highly intellectual, worldly, yet sensitive woman has come full circle in her psychic and sexual development. Her last statement clearly illustrates the validity of the point that Marion Woodman so forcefully makes in *Addiction to Perfection,* that "virginity for a woman is a state of mind, a way of being," that even a sexually jaded woman can be a "still unravished bride"[2] and can find and reawaken the Madonna aspect of her personality.

But sexual promiscuity and loss of moral discrimination are not the only symptoms of the collapse of the Madonna in the contemporary woman. Irritability, lack of patience, and a hard-edged, critical attitude are also symptomatic of loss of connection with this important aspect of womanhood.

"Male Bashing"

The feminist movement made many demands upon men. It certainly did not advocate any form of patience with them; in fact, it blamed men for everything. "Male bashing" become a favorite pastime among liberated women, who seemed categorically outraged with the opposite sex. Anger and scapegoating are natural and predictable responses when a person feels put upon by another. Feminist thinking suggested to women that they were being persecuted and suffocated by men, their lives restricted and their options limited. Little wonder that before long the opposite sex became the enemy, the scapegoat. And if one views the opposite sex as the enemy, one is not apt to exercise very much patience or tolerance in dealing with them. This has proven to be an inestimable loss to both men and women, for almost all men respond poorly to a woman who lacks serenity. Indeed, a woman without serenity seems hardly a woman at all; she is nervous, high-strung, all "bent out of shape," and utterly impatient.

Amazon Women won't wait for anything. They have too much to do, and they want to be the first to do it. Yet, in all of mythology, it is the maiden who waits. The knight comes to her and carries her off into the sunset of eternal togetherness. All women, even Amazons, dream of this. But in order to make it happen, a woman has to develop a certain passive-receptive attitude, a sense of patience.

"Delay of gratification" is a psychological concept that refers to the postponement of immediate pleasure for future good. The ability to delay gratification is considered to be one of the hallmarks of emotional maturity, both in men and in women. Most everyone agrees that patience is a virtue, essential to happiness; even the Bible says that "love is long-suffering." But the contemporary woman, always achieving and looking for trouble, has very little patience, very little ability to delay gratification.

It is interesting to note the plethora of books on the market devoted to the pursuit of pleasure by women. Some (*For Yourself* by Lonnie Barbach) are genuinely helpful and illuminating for the nonorgasmic or sexually repressed woman. Others (*Sex Tips for Girls* by Cynthia Heimel) are capricious in nature, separating sexual activity from all moral values and consequences, that is, separating the Courtesan from the Madonna.

Yet other books are more complex, integrating psychological and sexual issues with personal revelation. An example of such a book is *Sleeping with Soldiers: In Search of the Macho Man* by Rosemary Daniell. Ms. Daniell's tale is one of a forty-five-year-old woman who, having led a bourgeois life consisting of marriage and children, then seeks to choose her lovers for reasons of pleasure as opposed to shared values, thereby expressing a part of herself long held dormant (the Courtesan). Since Ms. Daniell has already been married three times and borne two children, her Mother-Madonna nesting instinct has been fulfilled. In the second half of her life, she chooses to plunge into the Dionysian depths of her psyche and "walk on the wild side" with actually very little to lose.

Ms. Daniell is an unusual woman, a woman of extremes in both the intellectual and erotic realms. The danger of such a book is not for the mature woman who has already experienced husband and children, but for the younger woman at a different time in her life. Unless the younger woman wishes to spend her life moving casually from lover to lover, she must readjust her consciousness to choosing her partners not on the basis of pleasure alone but upon shared values which can continue throughout a lifetime. Once addicted to pleasure, however, she may find this extremely difficult to do. The withdrawal symptoms from such a lifestyle can be as painful as withdrawal from any other substance that gives a quick high, such as heroin or cocaine. And many may not wish to withdraw at all. Still, in describing the end of her Don Juan period of hedonism, Ms. Daniell says, "I began to yearn to be part of two, to buy a lobster and cook it with someone I knew, someone with whom even after sex I might want to stay and talk a while."[3]

SEXUAL SPORTS

Once, I asked a pornographer to define sexuality for me. He responded, "Fucking is friction." Sounds coarse, but if a woman fails to utilize the Madonna aspect of her personality, then, indeed, that's all it is. And there are just so many ways that a man and woman can engage in this particular kind of friction and still find it amusing if there is no love attached to it. When there is affection, romance, and spirituality between a man and a woman, sex is not merely friction but an unending discovery and affirmation of love.

Without the Madonna—that is, spiritual values—in sex, the orgasm itself becomes the thing of value. Women and men both become obsessed with the "orgasm count" as a key to evaluating sexual experience. "How many times did you come?" assumes greater importance than "How did he make you feel?" These are values which must be dictated, however subtly or unconsciously, by the woman (even though it might not seem "fair"). Men are less sexually complex than women; they approach sex in a simple, direct way. They need women to set sexual standards, to "civilize" them. Otherwise, sex is just "friction" to them.

"Sportfucking" has become a popular colloquialism referring to casual sex as a sort of athletic event. For many contemporary women, relationships with men are competitive and contain elements of castration, for they have neither the time nor the inclination for genuine bonding or attachment to a man. Staying "on top," in control, is of paramount importance to them. Split off from their Madonna aspect without genuine feminine composure, receptivity, or serenity, these women conjure up images of a devouring, consuming monster, a Lady Macbeth completely divorced from her feminine feeling, a woman for whom power is more important than love. Not a very pretty picture . . .

The Amazon Woman's femininity is split off from her sexuality when she can't appreciate her lover beyond his ability to turn her on. Many such women tend to objectify men. Cut off from their deepest feelings and feminine instincts, they love to talk about sex, to be bold and lusty and very descriptive. Recently, I was at a party with a man I'd just started dating when an Amazon Woman whose acquaintance I'd just made came up to me and whispered, "I checked him out for you, and I hear he's a great lay."

In *Knowing Woman*, Irene Claremont de Castillejo points out that when women become masculine and men become feminine, each takes on the worst traits of the other. Men take on a woman's softness without her strength; women take on a man's toughness without his kindness.[4] I've observed this to be true in the modern woman, who has taken on the characteristics not of the best men, but the worst. She has a blue-collar-worker attitude in her sexuality and treats men as "things," comparing penis size and staying power with a lack of discretion that would shock even a longshoreman.

"I just get my rocks off and that's all" was the way in which D., a high-powered television producer, described her relationships with men. It was disconcerting to hear a woman using this uniquely masculine phrase for making love, imitating one of the worst aspects of masculinity: a vulgar approach to sex.

At a recent party, two young women, not crazed groupies but intelligent executive types, were discussing their taste in musicians. One spoke fondly of the light strumming touch from her guitarist lover; the other praised the percussive rhythm and dexterity of her drummer boyfriend. I couldn't help but wonder about the other "boys in the band" and imagined these women had tried them all.

For along with sexual freedom for women came

sexual experimentation of every sort. Women wanted to be "good sports." The Madonna aspect of personality fell out of favor in the 1970s. Women went to orgies, participated in odd sexual arrangements, accommodating to mostly male sexual fantasies that otherwise they would not even consider. Listen, for example, to my conversation with V., a contemporary woman of thirty-three who left her attorney husband some years ago and is extremely proud of her lack of sexual inhibition and her many wild and creative sexual antics:

"Sigmund Freud speculated that all women suffer to some degree from penis envy," I began. "Have you ever had any fantasies about this?"

"Well, actually no," replied V. "Not that I'm aware of. But I did try one on once."

"Really? Under what circumstances?"

"Well, I had a boyfriend who used to tell me that he had fantasies of having sex with men. But I always figured that they had been more than fantasies (he *had* been in the navy, after all), but I couldn't directly ask him. So one day, I went to the Pleasure Chest and got one of those strap-on dildoes. That night, we got very drunk on champagne. After we made love the first time, I went into the bathroom and put it on. I put a towel around my waist and came out of the bathroom and stood next to him by the side of the bed, and I said to him, 'How relaxed are you?' And he said, 'I'm pretty relaxed.' And I said, 'Are you *very* relaxed?' and he said, 'Yes, I'm very relaxed.' And I whipped the towel off and said, 'Then suck on this, baby.' He leapt across the room, and his mouth landed right on that thing, and he went crazy all over it. He loved it. Then I fucked him in the ass. He loved that even more. I loved it too. He grabbed his penis and had a violent orgasm as I was doing this. It was thrilling. He never asked me to do this again. But he loved me for it, I know he did. I was with him for three years."

"Then what happened to him?"

"Oh, he married a nineteen-year-old virgin from Mississippi. I guess he felt I had already done it all. He wanted a little girl. I guess he wanted to teach somebody."

Men do like to instruct women in matters of sex, for it gives them a sense of mastery and self-confidence. Some women may balk at this. But such women fail to understand that it is still the male of the species who is required to *perform* sexually; that is, to get and keep an erection. It can be argued that the secure man should not require "innocence" in his woman to ensure his sexual performance. And indeed, there are men who prefer a woman who has "been around." In general, however, I think this is not the case. Even the enlightened man whose reason tells him differently finds himself unconsciously repelled by the woman who is too experienced; in the dark depths of his unconscious mind, he wonders if he could ever trust such a woman.

Sexual trust is of paramount importance to a man; without it, he can never be sure that his children are his own. The woman, of course, is always sure that they are hers, for they are carried in her body. But it is only through his belief in his wife's sexual fidelity and virtue that a man can feel secure of the paternity of his children.

It should be pointed out, however, that virginity in the technical or physical sense is not what is being

discussed here, but virginity in the sense of purity of
spirit or soul. Many contemporary women with whom
I speak have lots of ideas about sexuality and relationship but no standards by which they live and
share their bodies. I am constantly getting calls from
women who don't know how to say no, who don't
even have the language for setting standards of any
sort, who are desperately afraid that if they do say
no, they will lose the men in their lives. Grown
women call asking if having sex with a certain man
at a certain time or in a certain way is "all right."
These women have lost touch with their own intuitive
sense of what's "right." They have neither feminine
virtue nor feminine values. As the feminist movement has glorified masculine values of power and
assertiveness, so it has overlooked feminine values of
relatedness and morality.

Uncommitted sex has not worked very well for
women. Many a woman has found that these liaisons
waste both her time and her energy, for uncommitted
sex is exhausting, not necessarily physically, but emotionally and psychologically. The next day, she doesn't
feel really good about herself and, as a result, often
doesn't look as good. She feels raped, not ravished.
A man might lose a whole night's sleep, but sex
usually puts him back at work raring to go. He's
"scored," while she's just "gotten laid." Whether
he likes the woman or not, a man almost always feels
powerful after sex. Yet whether she likes him or not,
a woman most often feels ambivalent. "Will he call?"
she wonders. "Do I even *want* him to call? If he
doesn't call, does that mean he doesn't respect me?"
If sex was good, she's eager to see him again and
hopes he shares her feelings. If sex was bad, she

feels degraded and hopes he'll stay out of her life. If sex was bad, but she likes him, she's desperate to see if she can make it better. Any way you slice it, the woman in an uncommitted sexual relationship is between a rock and a hard place.

It used to be that a woman had plenty of time to discover a man sexually. After all, she was having sex with her husband, or at least a husband-to-be. And even if the sex was less than perfect, she had the assurance that he would come back to her the following night. The single woman, however, in an uncommitted relationship lives in a perpetual state of uncertainty and anxiety.

THE MYSTIQUE OF THE MADONNA

Many women today wonder why they have such great difficulty in extracting commitments from men. The answer, of course, will vary from woman to woman. But in many cases it would appear that the contemporary woman has simply lost the mystique of the Madonna. She is "easy," she is available, she seems to have too few standards. Following her sensation, but not her intuition, she will have sex with a man before she gets any kind of commitment from him. She will live with a man, giving him what he wants and needs, before he has given her his complete devotion. For the woman with standards, playing "hard to get" comes naturally and is not a game, for she experiences herself as special and has values by which she lives. For the woman who is disconnected from her Madonna, however, there is little that is sacred about herself, her sexuality, or her femininity.

Such a woman has lost her feminine mystery; she has lost the mystique of the Madonna. She leaves her tampons and her douche bag lying around the bathroom, baring her most personal feminine secrets. She has an almost compulsive need to share her innermost thoughts and feelings with men in an effort to make them ''understand'' her. In reality, men often can't relate to and are absolutely overwhelmed by the feelings and needs of a woman because, by contrast, men are extremely simple creatures. Men think of women as unknowable, dark and exotic, moist and hidden; these elements are part of the excitement and allure of the ''feminine mystique,'' a mystique denigrated and rejected by early feminist leaders.[5] Yet the realm of the feminine has a power and reality separate and distinct from that of the masculine, which cannot be denied.

We live in a culture that emphasizes masculine performance values at the expense of human, loving, more feminine values. When a society such as ours elevates doing and denigrates simply being, it devalues the Madonna, the intuitive and spiritual part of woman and, indeed, of the entire culture. Perhaps its emphasis on masculine and patriarchal values is typical of a society in an advanced state of technology. The most primitive, nonindustrial cultures in the world, such as the aborigines of Australia and the Amish of Pennsylvania, are societies which greatly value the Madonna aspect of woman and the spiritual aspect of the universe. In other words, feminine values are emphasized above masculine values. Both the Amish and aborigine people have a highly developed sense of intuition. They have an enduring faith and trust that God will provide. In essence, they honor spiritual values above material accomplishment and consider the mechanization of modern civilization dangerous to the purity of the human soul.

PURITANISM AND PROMISCUITY

The Puritan ethic upon which this country was founded considered sex to be an act which one simply and absolutely did not perform except within the institution of marriage and solely for purposes of procreation. The sexual revolution dictated that sex ought to be explored anytime with anyone: If it felt good (even if it didn't feel *right*), one was supposed to do it.

At this point, neither of these two extremes feels comfortable to the contemporary American woman. She has discovered her sexuality and most likely does not want to postpone it until marriage. On the other hand, she is tired of casual liaisons and the empty, uncentered way they make her feel. Having moved from the extreme morality of Puritanism to the opposite but equally extreme feel-good ethic of the sexual revolution, she finds herself caught between one extreme and the other. She knows she must make choices that would fall somewhere in the middle—between Puritanism and promiscuity. But she doesn't know which choices to make. What the American woman must do is something that the European woman has been doing for years: She must integrate her Madonna and her Courtesan.

In looking for a life partner, most men seek a woman who somehow combines both equally powerful, yet practically opposite aspects of femininity. That is, they want "a lady in the living room, a whore in the bedroom.'' They respect the Madonna part of woman but delight in the Courtesan. The high standards of the Madonna do not put men off. Rather they act as an enticing challenge, making them want to ''lift the veil,'' to see how much fire burns underneath all that ice.

This ''Madonna-Prostitute Complex,'' first identified by Sigmund Freud, has been observed cross-culturally in men. But the integration of the Madonna and the Courtesan is especially difficult for the American woman, as she has wandered so far from her feminine center and her spiritual being. She has not only fallen off her Madonna pedestal, to her great despair and the despair of those around her; she has also lost touch with her skills as a Courtesan, sexualizing this aspect of femininity to the exclusion of its emotional and inspirational components.

The woman who embraces both the Madonna and Courtesan aspects of feminine personality is irresistible to men. Her Madonna is idealistic and unattainable; her Courtesan is visceral and enticing. Utilizing these two powerful aspects of femininity, women civilize and domesticate men, channel their sexual energies, and inspire them to greatness. It is women to whom men look to bring out their gentler natures and their highest ideals, inflame their passions, and motivate them to achievement. But this feminine woman is a rarity in today's culture, and the traditional male who still seeks valiantly for an inspiration or muse in his woman is apt to be bitterly disappointed.

How, then, might one become this truly ''feminine woman''? My readers may have noted, at this point, my omission of motherhood as an important element in my definition of the feminine woman. Ironically, in spite of the many hymns to "holy motherhood," I do not see the maternal aspect of female personality as central to the thesis of this book. It is true that many contemporary women have postponed motherhood for far too long, but, in fact, most women do continue to desire children. Maternal longings have not ceased simply because the contemporary woman has chosen, however unconsciously, to lean toward her masculine attributes and pursue power over love. On the contrary, her suppressed yearnings seem stronger than ever and are actively seeking expression.

But one must love a man before one loves a child. To love a man and truly bond with him, it is important first to redirect one's Amazon energies into the service of one's femininity, that is, to develop and integrate one's Madonna and Courtesan. It is to this subject that Chapter Five is devoted.

Embracing Femininity:
Melting the Amazon Armor

Woman is multifaceted, much like a diamond. Turn her this way, and she catches the light just so, reflecting one aspect of her personality. Yet, just like a diamond, turn her the other way, and you find what seems to be quite a different person. The changeability and variability of the female personality have been observed for so long that one can only conclude that this multiplicity of being is inherent in woman.

Ultimately, all women, to feel truly fulfilled, must throughout a lifetime integrate the many facets of their personalities, and each woman must do so in her own unique and individual way. There are, for example, still many women who need to embrace their Amazon aspects, developing their intellectual abilities and their assertiveness skills. These are the women who remain eternal girls, ever young, helpless, and dependent. But this is not the modern woman to whom I address this book, for even the average contemporary American woman is very much her own person. Having said so much in the negative about her, let us pause, then, and examine this extraordinary new Amazon Woman in a more positive light, for at her best, she is indeed a dazzling creature to behold.

The modern Amazon Woman presents herself in a

spectacular and dynamic way. She is articulate, in charge of herself and her world. Although her accomplishments vary greatly according to her motivation and training, she is for the most part self-sufficient and proud of her independence. She has developed her focused consciousness (though often at the expense of her diffuse awareness) and has learned how to set goals and meet them. Often this drive is excessive, for having so recently discovered her power, she can be overzealous in her utilization of it. She is curious about the world around her, eager to explore it, take risks, and have adventures. Her heightened consciousness and skills in the marketplace can be threatening to many men, for this woman is nobody's fool; she is a lady to be reckoned with.

The Amazon Woman is influential; what she has lost in the realm of the personal, she has to some extent made up for in the world of the impersonal, the larger, external body politic which has for so long been ruled only by men. While she still has a long way to go, it can safely be said that the modern Amazon Woman has indeed earned the respect and admiration of men. She has fought long and hard for her position in the world, and she is still fighting with courage—if with somewhat less idealism. She is younger-looking and more fit than any other generation of women, bearing children later in life, vital, athletic, and bursting with energy. There is no doubt that she has indeed "come a long way, baby." Against all sorts of odds, she has achieved unprecedented success.

But this is not a book about the success of the modern woman. This is a book that attempts to address some of her failures in the realm of the personal, issues which revolve around her alienation from her womanhood. There are many books already written about what the Amazon Woman has accomplished, and there are many others written about how she can accomplish more; that is, about how she can make it in a man's world. This book is not intended for that. This book is about how to make it in a woman's world. More specifically, it is about how the Amazon Woman can integrate her need for feminine fulfillment with the fact that her consciousness *has* been raised and that she *is* a person of accomplishment.

An "Unnatural Woman"

Many women today have expressed an earnest desire to reacquaint themselves with feminine modes of being vis-à-vis men and are frankly puzzled as to how to do so. Almost gone is the defensiveness, the anger, the addiction to outrage; today's woman has proven herself in the impersonal world and now wants to enter once again the world which is and has always been uniquely hers: the world of the personal. Simply put, women today are tired of being "one of the boys" and want to rediscover within themselves that which can only be called "the natural woman."

For the Amazon Woman is, in major respects, an *unnatural* woman. Working aggressively as she does in the marketplace, she is indeed often going against her nature, her monthly periods, the demands of childbearing and child-rearing, but, most critically, she is going against her nature in her relation to man, for her focused consciousness comes into direct conflict with his.

It must be remembered here that focused consciousness was earlier defined as a masculine way of being and thinking: goal-oriented, direct, and logical. That women can effectively mobilize this aspect of personality is today unquestionable, for they have done so. But at what price? What began as an effort to compromise and find a better balance through feminism has tilted so far the other way that today's woman knows only how to relate "man to man." This is in the nature of all revolutions, social, sexual, or political, the very word "revolution" being defined by *Webster's Ninth New Collegiate Dictionary* as "a sudden, radical, or complete change." By definition, then, a revolution is always excessive in nature. After revolution, there is inevitably a drawing back, not a drawing back to the point whence it started, but to some comfortable middle ground. Here is where the Amazon Woman stands today as she attempts to embrace some of the femininity which she has both consciously and unconsciously renounced.

The modern woman has discovered that living only through her masculine aspect has few, if any, advantages. The animus or thinking aspect of the woman, untempered by her feeling aspects, often runs rampant and tends to be excessive. Such a woman may seem lacking in simple humanity and may feel emotionally sterile and dry. It should be pointed out here that the man who is imbalanced in his masculine and feminine polarities suffers too; if tilted too severely toward his masculine aspect (the "macho man"), he seems a ridiculous caricature of maleness. If locked in the grip of his feminine aspect (his anima), he is at the mercy of his feelings and his moods. Such an "anima-possessed" male seems soft and passive in nature and has difficulty in taking charge of situations.

Psychologically healthy men and women require a balance between the masculine and feminine sides of their natures; the failure to integrate the masculine and feminine within results in an attempt to seek the "missing part" in someone else—in one's partner. Thus, the hard-edged animus-possessed Amazon Woman has a tendency to seek as her partner the soft and sensitive anima-possessed male, for all nature seeks a balance and the masculine *must* find the feminine, whether it be found in man or in woman. The Amazon Woman who is out of touch with her femininity will seek her feminine aspect in a man if she cannot find it in herself.

But it is usually more fulfilling for a woman when she embraces femininity within her *own* self and her *own* soul. Then, she feels differently about herself, about men, and about the world at large. Having embraced her loving and feeling capabilities, she begins to magnetize men who relate to her *as a woman*, not as a man, and these men are themselves more masculine in temperament, more protective and stable in their nature. In short, the feminine woman attracts the masculine man, and the woman thus becomes freed of many of the burdens of "being a man," as opposed to being a woman.

EMBRACING SERENITY

"Being a man," when one is, in fact, a woman, is tedious work; the woman who has not yet learned how to turn off her focused consciousness and slip easily into her diffuse awareness has a serious life problem. Such a woman is all "doing" and no "being," dynamic but not magnetic, aggressive and not receptive. She is often chronically fatigued by her unrelenting attempts to control and master her environment. From a psychological point of view, her behavior could be viewed as "obsessive-compulsive" in nature, i.e., rigid, controlling and restrictive. While obsessive-compulsive behaviors are highly effective in the workplace (they do get the job done), they are extremely limiting in one's range of personal and emotional experience, for such a focused and goal-oriented attitude in life suppresses natural joy and spontaneity. The obsessive-compulsive personality cannot just "let it be"; nothing is simply "allowed" to happen. Yet in order to embrace femininity, one must allow life to happen, one must learn how to surrender to those aspects of life which one cannot and should not attempt to control. It is here where the contemporary woman gets into troubled waters, for she finds herself attempting to control *everything*, both in work and in life, and, as a result, is often totally lacking in that most feminine of all qualities, serenity.

In Shakespeare's *The Taming of the Shrew*, Katherine, having embraced her femininity, describes the countenance of the unserene woman:

A woman moved is like a fountain troubled,
Muddy, ill-seeming, thick, bereft of beauty;
And, while it is so, none so dry or thirsty
Will deign to sip or touch one drop of it.[1]

Serenity, of course, is one of the hallmarks of the Madonna aspect of the female personality. It has been characterized in many ways: as a oneness with nature, as a feeling of connection with all living things, as an abiding faith in the rightness of the world, as a type of loving and patience which transcends reason.

But how to get there? There's the rub. Every day, women experiencing this difficulty ask me for guidance, and I am often somewhat at a loss as to how to guide them, for this is a process, not a product. Quiet meditation, long walks in nature, warm baths, dance, and involvement in artistic endeavors help to facilitate the process. But all these things take *time,* and time is the one thing that the contemporary woman is most often lacking.

A NEW WAY OF BEING IN THE WORLD

So how "liberated" are we really? Behind the perfect and self-contained facade of many a contemporary woman lies a stressed and unhappy individual who often feels she simply does not have time for actual living. Formerly chained to her home, her husband, and her children, she now is often chained to her work, to her goals, or to her (secret) food, drug, or alcohol addiction. The suppression of natural feminine feeling and serenity has taken its toll on modern woman, who is today feeling the pressure as never before and who yearns for release from this new oppression. I have often remarked that the "liberated woman" is *the one who gets what she wants,* and by this definition, few women today are truly liberated. One might begin this journey into femininity by asking oneself questions such as "Am I happy?" "Do I feel fulfilled?" "Do I have a sense of truly being alive and at peace in the world?" I believe that having answered these questions, many a warrior woman will feel ready to lay down her arms and consider a new way of being in the world.

There is no doubt in my mind that almost every Amazon Woman can greatly benefit by embracing her femininity. The choice as to whether she wishes to remain tilted toward her Amazon consciousness or develop her missing feminine parts is, of course, up to the individual woman. There is no question, however, that the embracing of femininity will make most women infinitely more desirable to men. More important, embracing femininity will make most women feel far more comfortable in their own bodies and in the world at large. And it is to these women who wish to rediscover this hidden and suppressed part of themselves that the remainder of this book is directed.

In this age of multiple choices for women, the range of what one can be, both professionally and personally, is wide. Some contemporary Amazon Women wish to remain as they are, having come to a point in their lives where they have made peace with themselves and do not seek or require this type of change. It is my strong impression, however, that large numbers of contemporary women are sincerely seeking a new way of being, a new way of experiencing themselves as women, and, in particular, a more fulfilling way of relating to men.

It has been argued that many of the characteristics of womanhood that I shall discuss in the second half of this book are "natural" or "instinctive" to woman; nonetheless, much of this naturalness has been obscured by the acquired masculine and dynamic behaviors promulgated by the individualism and feminism of the last decade. These skills and behaviors have served women well in their quest for power in the outside world but left many a bright, energetic, and successful woman alone and failing in her personal life. No matter how strongly such a woman attempts to justify her sense of ''self-actualization,'' in truth she often feels unfulfilled, not yet participating in real life. Since bonding with a man has not been a high priority in her life she has in fact paid little attention to it, assuming that it, and childbirth, and other assorted female preoccupations would simply take care of themselves. After all, it happened that way for our mothers, our grandmothers, and our great-grandmothers before them; why shouldn't it happen that way for us as well?

But, in truth, it hasn't. Our mothers and their mothers before them made a study and a career out of being a woman and invested themselves totally in this. As with any career, there was pleasure and pain, costs and trade-offs. The woman of yesteryear reaped many benefits, though often she paid a heavy price. Men, marriage, and children certainly did not come easily to her; she worked for them, sacrificed for them, gloried in them, and oftentimes lived through them. Hers was a world of love, not power.

Many women today wish to reenter this world of the feminine, at least to some extent, but are not certain exactly what they may have to give up in order to do so. They suspect that there are hidden treasures there, yet fear what they may lose in the pursuit of them.

''THE AUTHENTIC FEMININE''

So one returns again to the burning question of the hour, namely, *why* embrace femininity? Will ''melting the Amazon armor'' prove dangerous in the external world, leaving one vulnerable, defenseless, and exposed? This is, of course, the underlying fear of many modern women who have fought long and hard for their independence and equate their masculine strivings with strength and their feminine yearnings with weakness.

How, then, does one communicate the profound psychological and existential advantages of redeeming what the Jungians refer to as the "authentic feminine"?

The answer is as multifaceted as woman herself and perhaps must be experienced and deeply felt to be truly understood. Still, I am finding that many women who daily share their lives with me are already on this path, intuitively sensing that it will lead them home. The time they once claimed they did not have to "be a woman" they are now creating, and large numbers of them are shouting "enough is enough!"[2] Suddenly, the Superwoman is out of vogue, weary with battle fatigue. Women are slowing down at long last, returning to their natural rhythms, breaking out of their controlling animus possession with the same eagerness with which they once seized upon it.

And there is something charming and delightful and youthful about all of this. Sexually experienced women have grown "shy" with men, wondering what to do or say. For giving up control often uncovers a profound fear of dependency and vulnerability which was hitherto unrecognized. The Amazon Woman often discovers that her striving for achievement and excessive discipline has in fact all but obliterated the person she truly is, and discovering that person, the person at her feminine center, becomes an awesome psychological voyage.

Let us then begin. We have had enough psychological theory: animus, anima, focused consciousness, diffuse awareness. I have tried to state my case as clearly as possible, but I find, in the final analysis, that my listeners and callers want answers, not fancy psychological theory. Psychologists have a maddening tendency to overexplain and justify everything, and femininity requires no justification or explanation save the simple desire and fundamental yearning to embrace it.

BODY AND SOUL

I take biological motherhood for granted; motherhood is inherent in being *female,* though not inherent in being *feminine.* Many a man has called my radio program to say that he "loves" but is not "in love with" his wife, the mother of his children; many a mother has called to complain that she no longer feels "like a woman." For me, the essence of true femininity is captured in the aspects of personality which I have called the Madonna and the Courtesan, and the woman who develops and integrates these aspects of self will experience a profound change in her personality and her relationships with others. Perhaps the most remarkable aspect of this change will be the ease with which love enters her life, for feminine energy is not only powerful, it is also magnetic.

It can quickly be seen that the Madonna aspect of woman represents her soul, and the Courtesan her body, and the integration of these two polarities is no small task. As we go through the material which is to follow, however, bear in mind that one does not have to do any of these things all at once, and that "baby steps" or approximations to the ultimate goal of femininity are very much in order. Each woman must find her own balance and comfort level with this material, and it must be remembered that the ideal of femininity that I am presenting is just that: an ideal. Like all ideals, it is extreme in nature and not really the way that actual women are. Bearing this in mind, I have still found that this presentation is useful in guiding the uninitiated along this exciting and uncharted emotional terrain.

The Keeper of His Soul

We shall speak first of the Madonna or soul aspect of woman. This aspect of femininity is projected externally through a woman's outward radiance and sense of serenity, but must first be developed internally. There is nothing more attractive in a woman than the possession of a sense of true inner happiness, and one effective way to achieve this is through the embracing of a religious faith.

Carl Jung believed that an excellent way to begin the process of psychotherapy was by sending his analysands back to the religion of their birth; church or synagogue can indeed be a good place to find one's spiritual center, one's sense of connection with the universe. Traditional religion has been abandoned by many today, and New Age religions have sprung up to take its place. Any spiritual path chosen can be useful and comforting to the individual, for I am convinced, along with Jung and his followers, that there is something in man which cries out for connection with the universe at large. Women, in particular, are aware, however vaguely, of this connection, for they are the carriers of the race, the link without which life itself could not exist. This biological fact alone gives woman a unique sense of spirituality, and it is not an accident that it is usually the woman and not the man who insists upon some type of religious observance in the home.

This sense of spirituality is important, for it is the source of the Madonna's abiding *faith* in that which she cannot see or touch directly: faith in the future, faith in her man, faith in the goodness of life itself. Due to the current Crisis in the Madonna, life has become vastly impersonal for many women. Women have gone full scale away from a life devoted entirely to the personal, a life where a typical woman existed entirely in relation to others. She knew much, this woman of yesteryear, because she lived through her men and her children, and she was a powerful mediator of thoughts and feelings to those around her. Of course, the one person whom she often *didn't* know was herself. But in some ways she didn't need to; her role was so well defined by what she did for everyone else that she often had a very strong sense of self and personal fulfillment. This archetypal Medial Woman or Madonna was the center of the family and, in a profound sense, the very soul of the family. With the contemporary emphasis on career and economic independence, many women have forgotten that this Medial role vis-à-vis man is a source of great comfort, inspiration, and satisfaction to both sexes.

But this role is difficult for modern woman, for it

requires not only serenity and faith, but infinite patience as well. And the modern woman is lacking in patience; she has so much to *do* in the world. Women, of course, have always had much to do, but the demands of the marketplace are vastly different from the demands of the home. At home, there are pressures but no deadlines, unending tasks to be sure, but the ability to pace oneself as one wishes. The external world is different; one must toe the mark or fail at one's task. The masculine or focused consciousness is a driving one, linear in nature, moving toward its goal in a direct line and in as short a time as possible. The feminine consciousness, by contrast, is spiral in nature, enjoying the process as much as the product, moving through time in a leisurely way, allowing life to happen. This feminine attitude very much parallels the process of pregnancy and birth, which cannot be forced but must be allowed to happen in its own way.

Extended periods of silence, meditation, and contemplation are valuable in developing the Madonna aspects of personality, for the Madonna is, in large part, a *silent* aspect of woman. The Amazon aspect, by contrast, always has a voice, and often that voice can be strident and insensitive to the feeling tone of the environment. This occurs when the woman operates only out of her Amazon aspect without connection to her femininity; the results can be disastrous in an intimate or personal relationship, causing men to retreat emotionally and sexually. The woman who is possessed only by her Amazon intellect is not attached to her heart and her soul, and her excess verbiage builds a wall rather than a bridge between her and her man. This is why so many men often prefer the silent woman; in her silence they experience no barriers to her femininity, to the part of her that is quintessential woman. Often, the most profound communication between a man and a woman occurs in silence, for in silence the woman is totally receptive to the man, to his thoughts, to his feelings, and to his needs. My father used to say, "Silence is the severest form of intimacy."

Words are "productions" and require an effort of the mind. Often they interfere with affairs of the heart or workings of the soul. It is my feeling that one reason the Amazon Queen Hippolyta and the Greek King Theseus were able to make such a profound connection, in spite of their individual power, was because of their lack of a common language. Their verbal communication was extremely limited, forcing them to confront each other on levels other than the mind.

Therefore, in attempting to develop the Madonna, I advise many women to suppress their newfound capacity for verbal expression in their personal relationships with men. Women who have tried this new (yet very old) approach to male-female relationship find it awkward and uncomfortable at first, for the Amazon is accustomed to being "onstage," always performing. Silence often makes her feel fragile and vulnerable. It is initially difficult for her to "just be." Over time, however, she finds that "just being" is extremely pleasant, especially when her male companion so readily rushes in to fill the empty spaces.

But the Madonna does indeed speak, and when she speaks, she speaks softly. The voice of the Amazon is often loud and direct; the voice of the Madonna is soft and inviting. A shrill voice in a woman is anathema to men; it is sharp and cutting like a drawn sword, causing men to recoil or attack. Some fight back, others withdraw, but real communication seldom takes place when a woman is loud. The power of a soft feminine voice delivering a quiet yet determined message will usually freeze a man in his tracks and, if not force him to action, at least motivate him to think about what one is saying. Most men are frightened of a woman out of control; they simply do not know what to do under these circumstances. There are taboos against striking women, and most men don't. Yet if the woman presents herself in a loud and assaultive way, there is a natural desire on the part of a man to defend his maleness and strike back. The soft voice, on the other hand, lowers his defenses and enables communication to take place without impairing his dignity.

The literal translation from the Latin of the word "Madonna" is "my lady." Yet many contemporary women take no pride in being ladies and choose instead to imitate men. And in their attempt to be "one of the boys" many have inadvertently mimicked the language and behavior of the lower-class male, thereby imitating the culture and mores not of white-collar workers but of blue-collar workers. Between the sixties and the eighties women started talking like dockworkers, not only working like men, but acting and sounding like them. This jump down off the pedestal has been most disconcerting to men, as it separates a woman from her Madonna, the part of woman that men are raised to revere. Many men are taught early in life not to use obscenities in the presence of a lady; when the lady herself begins to swear, it violates his sense of her specialness.

Thus far, then, we have learned that embracing femininity via the Madonna aspect of personality involves patience, faith, and serenity, all of which can be experienced internally and projected in various ways. But my experience has been that this aspect of womanhood, however great its rewards, is extremely difficult for the modern woman to embrace.

As I write this chapter, my gaze wanders to a little red heart on my dressing table that says, "Love is patient." I use it as a reminder to slow down, to breathe deeply, to be kind, to not get too caught up in the world of power and achievement. Yet, like many Amazon Women, I have a real fear of slowing down, a fear that if I do, my world will crumble. And who will be there to pick me up? Theseus, where are you?

LOVE OR POWER: A DOUBLE BIND

This is a chronic dilemma for the modern woman: The more successful she is, the more intense her conflicts become. The more success she enjoys on the professional level, the less secure she often feels on the personal or emotional level. This reality of life for modern woman was predicted many years ago in "Femininity and Successful Achievement: A Basic Inconsistency," a classic study by Matina Horner, now president of Radcliffe College.[3] Dr. Horner discovered in her research that the brilliant and gifted Radcliffe women whom she studied had an uncanny fear of success, a fear which at the time was thought to be irrational. I believe time has proven that these fears were not irrational; these women intuitively suspected that high levels of accomplishment in the impersonal world might be detrimental to their happiness on a personal level. They accurately perceived the truth behind "Big Lie Number Three: Accomplishment Enhances Desirability," for in reality the reverse is often the case. When a woman embraces power over love, she usually must negate some aspect of her femininity, since the drive for power and the drive for love are polar opposites.

So what is one to do? The answer is, quite simply, anything one chooses. There is nothing in my judgment inherently wrong with the pursuit of power for men or for women. But I do think that it is important to communicate to women that if it is love they seek, it may be necessary to relinquish some of their power drives and start to embrace the world through the heart rather than the head. And the power of the heart is the power of love. This loving potentiality can be realized through the Mother, Madonna, and Courtesan aspects of female personality, the Madonna being the most patient and serene.

Before embracing femininity, my own Madonna was often severely deficient, so much so that years ago, a gentleman friend of mine remarked, "You leave the best part of yourself on the radio." The Madonna of a woman is severely tested on a daily basis, and the success or failure of a personal relationship will often revolve around a woman's ability to prevail in this aspect of her personality. A woman's Madonna aspect is perhaps most frequently challenged when a man is acting "unfairly" or is in a state of irritation or frustration. One option is to engage in battle with him, causing him to defend himself and become arbitrary and unyielding; the other is to maintain serenity, to rise above the situation and thereby give him something to admire in her. It is the rare man who has "the patience of a saint"; this quality is most often found in woman, and it is highly inspirational and motivational to man.

Listen to the story of A., a tall, dark-haired, exotic-looking advertising executive:

"I decided to flex my Madonna muscles with my new boyfriend," reported A., who had been working very intensely on a project that involved her putting in very late hours at the office. Her new boyfriend, H., a stockbroker, had expressed interest in marrying her (much to the delight of A., who was thirty-seven and had never married) but was quite distressed by her unusually heavy work schedule. Formerly, A. had only had relationships with inadequate men, who had asked very little of her as they were way beneath her station in life; they were quite willing to fit into the small spaces of her hectic professional life and never complained about her working too much. H., on the other hand, was more of an "Actual Man," a man with his own busy work schedule. Though he admired and respected A.'s career, he very strongly desired that she be available to him when he wanted to be with her. A., not wanting to give up her work or her man, called upon the mediating powers of her Madonna aspect to help her through this conflict.

DIFFUSING OUTRAGE

"One night, I came home from work at two A.M.," she recalls. "All I wanted to do was curl up with H. in bed, talk, play, sleep together, maybe have sex, it didn't matter as long as we could share these few hours together before I had to go to work again the next day. When I came in, there he was, working on his portfolio. He looked at me coldly, said hello, made some crack about my being a slave to my work, then announced that he was going out—for no particular reason except that he felt 'claustrophobic' and 'wanted some air.' Going out at two A.M. when I'd just walked in the door! I was outraged! And in the old days, I would have expressed my outrage immediately. 'How *dare* you!' I would have screamed and started a big fight with him. But I remembered our discussion last week about silence and I decided, for a change, to say absolutely nothing. I just took a deep breath and tried to calm myself down as if I were my own mother calming down the part of me that is a big baby and cries when she's not getting her way.

"H. looked at me very strangely—I think he was surprised that I wasn't screaming at him for this—and asked me if I was upset. I took another deep breath and very slowly, very softly told him that I wasn't upset (by this time, I was so calmed down that I really wasn't!), but that I was *disappointed*, that I was very much looking forward to spending time with him and it was too bad that he was going out just as I was coming in. I could see his whole expression warming and softening as I spoke in this way. It was as if he'd been steeling himself to grapple with a mountain lion, and instead a little bird of paradise had landed on his shoulder."

Men react much better to a woman's silent disappointment than to her venting her anger. No woman can win in relationship with a man when she is doing battle. The overt expression of anger is challenging in nature, and is likely to be met with aggression, stubbornness, or withdrawal. Silence, on the other hand, or the simple expression of disappointment inspires kindness in a man and motivates him to reevaluate his own actions, which are often impulsive.

"Well, he went out anyway," continues A. "I guess he was just too proud to change his mind on that one. But he came back within half an hour, and we had the sweetest, warmest night together that we'd had in days."

SHEATHING THE SWORD

One of the more difficult challenges in developing the Madonna is to remain silent in stressful situations when many of a woman's Amazon instincts suggest that she should aggressively intervene. However, taking a few moments of silence will not only earn her the admiration of her lover, it enables her to evaluate her feelings, his position, the entire situation; it really gives her a chance to think before she speaks. In *Knowing Woman,* Irene Claremont de Castillejo refers to the "swordlike," castrating quality of the Amazon's outspoken, unrestrained animus when it is not in touch with her feminine center.[4] Most women have an intuitive, primitive sense of exactly how to castrate a man when they are angry. Men know this, and appreciate it when a woman refrains from using this most deadly weapon, especially when they know they are wrong.

Castration is a man's greatest fear, and will be discussed at great length in Chapter Seven. Suffice it to say for the moment, however, that this very primitive fear manifests itself psychologically in what often appears to be an almost overbearing sense of pride in man. "Fair" or not, a woman in love must deal with this aspect of man, and it is here where her Madonna truly comes to her aid. Learning to keep one's voice low and controlled across a wide range of circumstances is not a Madonna task for the faint of heart, for it requires patience and mind control of the type that the Amazon Woman is used to exercising only in the marketplace. The contemporary woman has indeed learned to bite her tongue in business; she doesn't want to cut off the hand that feeds her, the hand which formerly belonged to a man but now belongs to her boss (male or female). Indeed, the respect which women formerly showed to their husbands and lovers has now been transferred to various individuals whom they admire professionally in the marketplace. In the work arena, women have come to realize that the proper respect will deliver its just rewards. The same is true in the arena of love, but alas, today this is viewed as "deferring" to a man, a deadly sin, a betrayal of the women's movement, indeed of one's very self-respect.

Yet many report to me that the embracing of the Madonna, in fact, *enhances* their self-respect and gives them a feeling of mastery over both themselves and their men. The woman who "tries on" these Madonna-type behaviors may at first feel uncomfortable, but will soon feel exhilarated at their value in her life—both personally and interpersonally. The Amazon armor worn so long by modern woman has proven unusually claustrophobic, shutting out much of woman's innate capacity for altruism and for loving in its purest form.

But the woman who embraces her Madonna without embracing her Courtesan might as well be a nun, for ultimate femininity must include the body as well as the soul. If the Madonna is a white light, the Courtesan is a red heat; the former inspires, the latter excites. Let us proceed, then, to examine this aspect of womanhood which Toni Wolff called the Hetaira, or "companion to man."

THE COURTESAN: A MAN'S WOMAN

What does it mean, truly, to be a "companion to man"? As with the Madonna, I shall explore this aspect of womanhood in its idealized form. By presenting to my readers the Courtesan in the extreme, one can get a better sense of what this aspect of womanhood really is.

The first thing that could be said about the Courtesan woman is that she is not her own woman, not a woman's woman, but a *man's woman*.

To be a man's woman, it is necessary to know how to be all things to all men, and in order to do this, one must know something about male psychology, as well as understand exactly what it is that men expect of women. For men evaluate women and have expectations of them which are different from those of other women and certainly different from those which women have of themselves. To see women *through a man's eyes* is very different from seeing women through a woman's eyes. And the woman who wishes to develop the Courtesan aspect of her personality must learn to adapt herself to a man in such a way as to fulfill his view and expectation of her.

To primitive woman, this came easily; she lived only in relation to man, bore his children, and was dependent upon him for fulfillment of her needs. This, of course, is no longer true of modern woman; her hard-won independence and self-sufficiency have made her not only unwilling but in many cases unable to adapt to man in the way that she formerly did. And yet, unconsciously and in spite of herself, modern woman *does* continue to adapt to man, for even the most aggressive Amazon Woman, when in love, seeks to please man, to arouse his passions, and to inspire his continuing interest in her. The woman in a love relationship with a man, then, will instinctively utilize some aspect of her Courtesan, usually without her awareness.

A Work of Art

Unlike the Madonna, the Courtesan is not other-directed, but self-centered. This may come as a surprise to those who view adaptation as the negation of self; on the contrary, adaptation to man, as viewed by the Courtesan, is extremely *self-serving*. The Courtesan views herself as a work of art, painting and displaying herself in such a way as to best enhance her natural beauty and fulfill the feminine ideal of the opposite sex. In Jungian terms, she has perfected the art of seizing or capturing the "anima projection" of the male; that is, she brings to life his idealized view of femininity.

In doing so, the Courtesan often plays a role, a role which is not necessarily consistent with other aspects of her personality. She does not mind this role, however, for she gets much satisfaction and pleasure from it, and her rewards are many: social, sexual, emotional, and financial. On the psychological level, it can be said that the Courtesan often seems to best experience herself and her life as deeply meaningful *only* when in relation to man, and while many a contemporary woman recoils at this notion, I believe there are just as many who secretly feel this way.

The woman who wishes to embrace her Courtesan must be willing to operate on two levels, the first being the level that men expect her to fulfill, the second being the level upon which she truly experiences herself as a person. In earlier times, the first level was the only one she dared manifest in behavior. The second level was secretly felt, never publicly displayed. Nowadays, things are different. A woman expresses freely the person that she feels she is and often adamantly refuses to adapt to the role men expect of her.

To Love or Not to Love

Herein lies the central conflict which many contemporary women experience and which is possibly the most common reason so many modern women are successful but alone. To love is in many ways to fulfill a woman's nature; yet, paradoxically, *not* to love is often to most fully be herself. In loving, it is important to note that one does not necessarily fulfill one's complete potential or express one's total self. Indeed, there is often much of the woman's true self that is ignored by her man (much to the woman's distress), at least until the lovers are deeply involved over a long period of time. What men actually want from us and how they see us is rarely consistent with who we actually are and how we see ourselves. In fact, it could even be argued that it is only when women do *not* love that they can most fully develop their unique talents and individual personalities, for loving takes time, energy, and attention to the needs of others. Still, few women envy the single or "barren" woman, and most secretly pity her, for they see her as somehow incomplete.

The Courtesan operates easily on these two levels and enjoys the results of her artful wiles to the utmost. She dresses to emphasize the differences between herself and men; her clothing is oriented toward form, not function, and is designed to show off her softness and fragility as opposed to man's hardness and strength. Skirts and dresses, soft fabric, lace, pastel colors, bows, ribbons, and other female paraphernalia are useful in creating this contrast between men and women. Note that these differences are merely *emphasized* by these accoutrements, not *created* by them, for women are already softer and more fragile than men in terms of their brute strength, weight, size, and muscle mass. On a strictly physiological level, of course, women are, in fact, hardier than men and enjoy greater longevity. But to the Courtesan, this is not the point. Her goal is to inspire tenderness, protection, eroticism, and passion in her man, and her projection of delicacy, femininity, and grace serve this purpose extremely well.

"JUST SHOW UP AND LOOK BEAUTIFUL"

All of the Courtesan's behaviors are designed to emphasize the differences between herself and the man, thereby enhancing his feelings of potency or strength. While in her Courtesan aspect, the woman does not attempt to demonstrate her self-sufficiency (however self-sufficient she may well be) by picking up checks, opening her own doors, or "making arrangements" of any kind. I am reminded of an incident some years ago when I was attempting, in typical Amazon fashion, to orchestrate an evening; finally, my escort silenced me by quietly saying, "All you have to do is show up and look beautiful."

The Courtesan does indeed attempt to enhance her individual beauty and her sex appeal, and there are many books devoted to this subject. Often, however, intangible aspects of femininity are not addressed: the sparkle in a woman's eyes, the radiance in her smile, the warmth of her laughter. The woman wishing to embrace the Courtesan aspect of her personality must master the art of communicating through her eyes, her smile, and her voice.

It is helpful to practice communicating feelings to a man nonverbally. A woman might try thinking erotic thoughts and projecting them only through her eyes, radiating her pleasure in his company through her smile and her laughter. It must be emphasized that the Courtesan aspect of woman, unlike the Madonna, is not serene, but vibrant and alive. Since this vibrancy must be translated and projected physically, cosmetics are extremely helpful, for they lend color, warmth, and sensuality to a woman's countenance.

MUSE TO MAN

It can easily be seen that the Courtesan aspect of woman is *designing* by nature, that is, it always seems to have one eye on the effect it produces. It is almost as if the woman, while in her Courtesan aspect, does not experience herself directly, but rather through the response she produces in others. Because of this, she often seems lacking in authenticity; i.e., there is something "unreal" about her. This, however, is rarely seen by men, only women, especially women who refuse to embrace this aspect of femininity. Yet there are tremendous rewards, biologically and psychologically, in "capturing the man's anima projection," becoming the *femme inspiratrice*, the muse to man. However contrived or artificial it may appear, it is still the Courtesan aspect of woman which attracts the male of the species. From an evolutionary point of view, this aspect of woman must be viewed as natural and instinctive.

Many people think of the Courtesan aspect of personality as dark, sultry, tempestuous; Carmen is an excellent example of this kind of Courtesan. But the Courtesan does not always present herself in this way; sometimes she is girlish or coquettish in nature, much like Marilyn Monroe. Whatever her presentation, and it can vary greatly, there is always an element of teasing or flirtation about her. This aspect of woman knows how to *play* with men, to diffuse the seriousness within them, to bring out what Eric Berne referred to as the "Natural Child."[5]

In transactional analysis, Berne identified three ego states within the person: the Parent, the Adult, and the Child. The Parent is the center of the attitudes and values, the Adult is the center of the thinking, and the Child is the center of the feelings. Many contemporary women have difficulty with the latter, fearful that the little girl within them will burst forth, making them appear foolish. In fact, the little girl within the woman is a natural and special part of her personality, just as is the little boy within the man. It is on this level, the level of the Child, that a man and a woman play together, laugh together, and experience a wide range of feelings, including sexuality. It is here, in the ego state of the Child, where we are most vulnerable, most exposed, and, on a purely emotional level, most ourselves. In fact, it can safely be said that one cannot truly know another individual intimately until one knows the little boy or little girl within.

GIRLISH CHARM

The Courtesan is not the least bit inhibited about displaying the girlish or childlike side of her personality. Notice here that I am using the word "childlike" as opposed to "childish." Childlike behaviors are disarming, open, natural, enchanting. Childish behaviors are immature, demanding, insensitive, and distancing. Even the most independent, autonomous, and self-sufficient woman does have a childlike aspect to her personality and can learn to project her girlishness, however foolish she may feel at first. In order to do this, however, the woman must be willing to trust the man she is with, for the Child is the *dependent* part of the personality.

All human beings have dependency needs, but modern woman has been loath to project her need of man in any way. This failure of modern woman to own and acknowledge the passive-dependent aspect of her personality has resulted in serious dysfunction and alienation between the sexes. The woman's denial of what is, in fact, a very real part of her results in her being autonomous but alone, bereft of male protection and care, for her behavior has inspired none. Frequently, in the dead of night, she awakens in a panic, the frightened little girl within crying out for comfort and reassurance.

These problems diminish greatly when a woman develops the Courtesan aspect of her personality. In acknowledging her need of man, her need for his strength, protection, and comfort, she becomes not a weaker, but a stronger person. Jung has pointed out that any time an aspect of personality is relegated to the background, it becomes what he called an "inferior function." This inferior function or "shadow" part of the personality has a strange and disabling effect upon the individual. The fact that an aspect of personality is unconscious does not mean that it is powerless. On the contrary, it is the unconscious aspects of personality that usually have the most power, for they creep up on us and affect our lives without our awareness or conscious control.

The fact that women have been overwhelmed by their repressed dependency needs can be seen by a brief examination of the plethora of popular books which address this subject in one way or the other: *Smart Women, Foolish Choices, Women Who Love Too Much, Why Do I Think I'm Nothing Without a Man?, Men Who Hate Women and the Women Who Love Them,* and others. That unpleasant word "desperate" must be used here, for women today *are* desperate to be with men but do not know how to relate to them so as to inspire their protection, their devotion, their love, and their care. According to these books, it is the male who is at fault. Yet the world simply cannot be filled with so many bad men, nor could today's highly intelligent woman be making so many "foolish choices" without cause. I strongly believe that it is the failure of modern woman to effectively utilize the unique power of her femininity —a power which is easily within her reach—that results in so many disastrous and loveless relationships.

SHOW HIM THAT YOU NEED HIM

The modern woman has denied her Courtesan aspect and hidden her dependency needs behind her Amazon armor. An important part of melting the Amazon armor is reaching out to men and showing them that you *need* them. This can be done in a variety of ways, but the wisest and most direct is simply to *ask for their help*. Do not relate "man to man"; ask for help as a little girl might, sweetly and politely, as in "Will you please?" This attitude allows a mature man to feel strong and important; most Actual Men would not dream of refusing such a request. The help could be of a physical kind ("Will you please help me move this piece of furniture?"), emotional ("Will you please help me get through this situation?"), intellectual ("Will you please help me understand what is going on here?"), or material ("Will you please take me out to dinner tonight?"). The largeness or smallness of the issue at hand is of no importance; in fact, asking for advice in small matters is just as effective as in large. The point is that the Courtesan has no trouble in requesting what she needs of men and showing that she indeed *has* some needs. Again, it should be emphasized that the woman does not have to *invent* these needs, for she inevitably has them; she has only to learn how to express these needs properly and without embarrassment or shame. That this is difficult for the contemporary woman is beyond question; she has so long hidden behind her Amazon armor that she hardly knows how to relinquish her defensive system even when she wishes to.

Many of my callers report to me that they are aware that they somehow "intimidate" men, but don't quite understand why. They attempt to be attractive, engaging, warm, witty, interesting, and so forth. Yet the man fails to show continuing interest. A typical example is a recent call I received on my radio program from a divorced woman of forty-one who was having difficulty sustaining relationships. She reported that men tended to take her out for perhaps two or three months at the most, after which time they stopped seeing her. In at least three cases, she said that the men had said something to the effect of "You're too beautiful and you're too intelligent."

I pointed out to her that the possession of beauty and intellect could hardly be considered a liability on the battlefield of love and, if anything, should be considered an asset. And indeed, upon further questioning, it appeared that her beauty and intelligence were major magnetizing factors and initially proved extremely attractive to men. Yet further questioning soon revealed her overstriven self-sufficiency. The actual reason that this woman failed to keep her men was that she was personally uninspirational to them. What she projected to men was simply that she did not *need* them. Her beauty and intelligence were attractive; her independence and self-sufficiency were a turnoff. It is important that a man feels that he fulfills a purpose in your life, that he somehow makes the woman feel better, safer, and more beautiful than she was before. In short, he needs to know that his masculine presence makes a difference to her feminine being, otherwise two people may have met person to person, but not man to woman.

READY FOR LOVE

Sexually, the Courtesan aspect of woman is highly complex, intuitively sensing her man's needs and moods. She is at home in her body and ready for love. Nonetheless, she seldom initiates sex directly, for she understands that it is the man, not the woman, who must be highly motivated to engage in the sexual act, as it is the male of the species who has to perform. And motivate him she does, in her dress, her appearance, and her manner, for this woman knows how to use her hands, her eyes, and her body to maximum erotic advantage. Perhaps the greatest motivator of all is her wanton behavior in the bedroom and her frank pleasure in sex. This woman is not shy, and her man takes great delight in her responsiveness to him.

It has been said that orgasm is a necessity for men, a luxury for women. Without male ejaculation, the species could not be continued; a woman, by contrast, can be stone-cold and still conceive a child. Many women despair that they do not seem to be orgasmic every time they engage in lovemaking, and the current literature seems to suggest something terribly wrong with this woman, with her man, or with the overall quality of the relationship. This is not always so. A woman is highly distractible sexually, and the slightest interruption can break her mood and prevent her from climaxing. One often has the impression that it would take nothing less than a train passing through the bedroom to distract a man in the throes of passion; this is simply one of the many differences between the sexes.

The Courtesan is indeed orgasmic, but does not worry about it. Because of this, she is, in fact, more orgasmic than most women, yet when she fails to achieve orgasm, it is of little consequence to her. She has still enjoyed sharing the act of love and the passion and closeness it has engendered between her and her man. Since her desire is to continue to inspire her man's passion and enthusiasm, both for her and for their sexual contact, she seldom expresses disappointment. She is certainly not a masochist, for, as we have seen, the Courtesan is extremely self-serving. She does this simply because she understands that negativity has no place in the bedroom. In addition, unlike the Amazon, this woman does not feel compelled to share her every thought and feeling with her man; she has a private world, all unto herself, and is very much in charge of it. If her man needs teaching, she will teach him, but always through emphasizing what he does right, not what he does wrong. In psychology, this is known as positive reinforcement, and it has been irrefutably demonstrated that behaviors which are rewarded or "positively reinforced" are learned and retained at a much higher level than those which are not.

The Courtesan *creates* good lovers, and all men are better lovers for having been with her. Perhaps her greatest skill is in slowing men down and teaching them the *art* of love, and she does this not so much through direct instruction as through her frank expression of pleasure in many aspects of lovemaking which he may view as merely preliminary to "the act." And although she ultimately gets what she wants from her man, she is essentially nondemanding, for she knows that when women demand sex of men, the entire experience starts to feel like work to them. Over the years, many men have complained to me that sex had begun to feel like "a job," and this is understandable, for all performance on demand is experienced as work, not love. Sexual performance motivated by passion, however, is never viewed as work; it is a joy.

SAINT AND SINNER: THE BEST OF BOTH WORLDS

From the brief descriptions given so far, it can be seen that the Madonna and Courtesan aspects of womanhood, though equally enticing to men, are diametrically opposed in nature. *Yet all men fervently desire to find these two aspects in one woman.* The Madonna without the Courtesan is a saint; the Courtesan without the Madonna is a whore. Most women, of course, do not live at these extremes of their personalities and do find some sort of middle ground. But it is the rare woman who succeeds in integrating both the Madonna and Courtesan aspects of her personality in her daily life with the same man. Thus we have the emergence of what Sigmund Freud first identified as the "Madonna-Prostitute Complex," the tendency in man, universally observed, to view women as one way or the other. Frequently after marriage, and especially after childbirth, the man will imbue his wife with all sorts of Madonna-like characteristics, relegating her Courtesan to the background. And the wife often aids and abets this process, for she is physically fatigued and her attention has been diverted to her newfound role of motherhood. Often a couple never moves out of this phase, and the man and the woman both remain unfulfilled in their intimate lives. This splitting of the Madonna and Courtesan can be found in many cultures; in France, the mistress is an accepted part of the culture privately, if not publicly; in Spain, we have La Casa Grande and La Casa Chiquita, the large home of the wife and the little home of the kept woman.

But how limited in scope is the life of the woman who chooses to embrace only one of these aspects of femininity. She misses much, as does her man. Surely one of the aims of the well-lived life is to be all that we can be, both to ourselves and to the ones we love. Melting the Amazon armor and embracing femininity through the integration of the Madonna and the Courtesan is the beginning of a fascinating and complex journey into womanhood. The woman who does so will experience profound changes both psychologically and physically: tightness leaves the face, hardness is replaced by softness, tension by relaxation. Often lifelong physical disabilities disappear as if by magic. But most exciting, the woman starts to recognize that she is magnetizing men, men of a new and different kind, and from these men, she is then able to choose her hero, the subject of our next chapter.

CHAPTER SIX

Finding Your Hero: Magnetizing Your Man

The concept of "man as hero" lives deep in the unconscious of all women, even today. Modern women have struggled long and hard to find the hero within themselves, yet, contrary to Gloria Steinem's edict, we have *not* "become the men we wanted to marry." Indeed, we have not become men at all but have remained women with the same atavistic longings and needs of women everywhere. Women today are frankly acknowledging their need of men, and are attempting in various ways to embrace their femininity and establish intimate connections with the opposite sex.

Over the past year, I've noticed a marked shift in the wind; the casual affair is no longer in vogue, sexual experimentation is definitely passé, and a recent issue of *Cosmopolitan* (November 1986) had several pages of photographs of young mothers and their babies. No question about it: Marriage and motherhood are "in," and many a modern woman has laid down her Scythian sword, divested herself of her Amazon armor, and found contentment with the hero of her choice. Yet many women remain alone, in spite of their efforts toward bonding. Relationships fail; no man ever seems quite heroic enough. Often, what has happened is that these women have fallen in love with the man within themselves, an aspect of the animus which M. Esther Harding has appropriately named "The Ghostly Lover."[1]

THE GHOSTLY LOVER

Harding first described the Ghostly Lover in her classic study of female psychology entitled *The Way of All Women*, first published in 1933. The Ghostly Lover can most simply be seen as the great *him*, the perfect man, Mr. Right, Mr. Wonderful, that man—real or imaginary—that a woman can never have, the Prince Charming that is sure to arrive—someday—on her doorstep, glass slipper in hand. The Ghostly Lover may be a real man, a man she has loved and lost, a love that can never be. Or he may be an ideal, a figment of the woman's imagination.

In psychological terms, the Ghostly Lover is an exalted and unrealistic animus projection; it is as if the woman takes the male within herself (her animus), idealizes him, and projects that ideal out onto every man she meets. In a very real sense, the Ghostly Lover is the personification of the woman's tendency toward grandiosity. He is her perfect male self. Needless to say, real men cannot meet this test; almost all men fare poorly when compared with a woman's Ghostly Lover.

The woman possessed by her Ghostly Lover involves the men in her life in a destructive psychological game called Blemish, described by transactional analyst Eric Berne in his popular book *Games People Play*.[2] Berne defines a psychological game as a transaction between two human beings which seems simple and direct in nature but has an underlying and often unconscious ulterior motive; the ulterior motive beneath the "blemish" game is the destruction of intimacy. Women who play "blemish" are always finding fault: "He'd be perfect *if only* he were taller, shorter, richer, smarter, wittier," and so forth. No man is ever quite right, and the woman remains "married" to an idealized man, the Ghostly Lover in her head.

The Blemish player often doesn't even realize she is being critical. Her Ghostly Lover is a demon master; jealous of her attempts at intimacy with real men, he holds the woman fiercely in his grip. He serves as a barrier between her and real life, thereby reinforcing her self-sufficiency and keeping her trapped in her "when" script. *Real* life—and love and marriage and motherhood—will begin, she tells herself, "when" she meets the *right man*. But the right man never comes along, for every man has a blemish, a flaw, an imperfection which is somehow intolerable, especially when compared to the ghostly image of masculine perfection that hovers in her unconscious.

During the teenage years, it is normal for women to have fantasies of a dream lover; most women grow up with fairy-tale princes on their minds. But growing into womanhood means bonding with an *actual* man and loving him for exactly what he is, not what one wishes he could be. If the power of the Ghostly Lover does not wane but grows stronger as a woman ages, his hold on her becomes so powerful that soon no man can bond with her, for she is indeed "married" to the Ghostly Lover within.

UNWED AND CHILDLESS

Criticism of men, commonly known as "male-bashing," steadily grew through the feminist and sexual revolutions, and with it, so did the Ghostly Lover within modern women. Women did not give up on men; they simply expected *more* of them. And the more women expected, the less adequate men seemed. Suddenly, no man was a hero; how could he be? Woman was the new hero, seized by her own sense of specialness, deluded by the psychological grandiosity discussed in Chapter One as "Big Lie Number Four: The Myth of One's 'Unrealized Potential.' " No longer was man looked to for security, strength, and protection. The modern woman sought these virtues within herself. Men, by comparison, often seemed weak and ineffectual; it was difficult to view them as heroic, for women were often surpassing them in the world of money, power, and status.

Or so it seemed. Sylvia Hewlett, in her brilliant analysis of the economic and social condition of the modern woman, aptly entitled *A Lesser Life: The Myth of Women's Liberation in America*,[3] points out that women have failed miserably in their efforts to compete with men, not because they are less adequate intellectually but simply because they are women and have women's needs. In its 1982 study, *The Wall Street Journal* found that 48 percent of the women executives polled were married, as compared with 96 percent of the men; and 52 percent of these women executives were childless, as compared with only 7 percent of the men.[4]

These are grim statistics for women. Simply translated, it can be seen that roughly half of the top female executives remained single, and, of those who did marry, half remained childless. Only 25 percent of these top female executives, then, managed to combine career, marriage, and children.

Perhaps these top Wall Street executive women, childless and alone, have no regrets, for many of them have, in fact, married their Ghostly Lovers in the form of their work; as such, work becomes the recipient of all the woman's instinctual and libidinal energies. The Ghostly Lover operating in this way is not necessarily destructive, but indeed can be quite positive, especially if the woman's work is character-ized by a sense of dedication and sincere involve-ment. Work of this nature has the characteristics of a "calling" and may be experienced as fulfilling on many levels. The woman becomes one unto herself, and if there are men in her life, they operate in a secondary capacity, for these women have learned the extent to which loving can be a distraction.

Even a dedicated woman, however, often contin-ues to fantasize about her Ghostly Lover, a great King Theseus who will come and sweep her away when she is "ready." This fantasy is not particularly dangerous (and may even have some basis in reality) if the woman already has many of her feminine tasks behind her. Women who have already married and borne children may indeed not be in a state of readi-ness for renewed bonding, and may well afford to wait for a Theseus to come at a later time.

The Blemish game and the "when" script, how-ever, have proven to be extremely dangerous and nonproductive life patterns for the younger woman, who often finds herself unwed and childless at the height of her career. Modern woman, thinking that she was freed from her biology by contraception and legalized abortion, has discovered that her conflicts are greater than ever. Biology no longer has to be destiny, but to ignore it completely does not work very well either.

How did it happen that thousands of American women, in an attempt to deny the reality of their gender, marched into the work force like men and tried to become their own heroes?

"Any Fool Can Scrub a Floor"

It has already been stated that the modern American woman's sense of grandiosity was fostered in large part by feminism and the media. But many contemporary Amazon Women were also inculcated with this sense of "specialness" by their own mothers, who vicariously lived out their dreams and ambitions through their educated and liberated daughters.

Many of the mothers of the past generation were strong Mother-Madonna types, extremely feminine women who raised extremely masculine daughters. Characteristically, this Mother-Madonna type woman was narcissistically involved with her Amazon-Courtesan daughter and was attempting to complete her own personality through her. This mother wanted the best for her child, and often her sense of the "best" was something other than that which she had experienced herself. Often she failed to communicate the pleasures of married life to her daughter and instead emphasized the world of achievement and intellect. "Any fool can scrub a floor," my own mother used to say to me. "Go read a book instead."

Later in life, however, this very same mother is

often the first to proclaim distress at her daughter's excessive independence and lack of a husband. In classic double-binding fashion, she pleads fervently for her daughter to marry and bring her grandchildren, yet often in some way negates every marital opportunity which presents itself. In unconscious collusion with her daughter's Ghostly Lover, the Amazon Woman's mother may actually feel that no *real* man is good enough for her very special daughter. One of my former patients, a wealthy, thrice-divorced self-made businesswoman with a highly symbiotic relationship with her mother (a Mother-Madonna type who has been married to the same man for fifty years), described the devastating effect of this upon her romantic life:

"Even after all these years, my mother is still telling me not to 'throw myself away.' With the truly inadequate men I've been with—and I've been with quite a few—I can certainly understand her point. But with others, it remains a mystery. If the man is much older, I'm throwing myself away because he couldn't possibly bring me the sexual satisfaction I require, and I'd have to see him through old age and death. If he's unattractive, then there are the physical negations. If he makes less money than I, then it's 'What do you need him for?' The men who want to share with me, i.e., the ones who are peers, are seen as invading my territory (which is substantial), and the ones who are very rich are usually also very dominant, and she objects to this also. I may be somewhat grandiose about my person, but not nearly so much as my mother. She has often said, in fact, 'I'd be the first to admit that in my judgment *no man is good enough for you.*' "

These excessively high expectations in love and in work put the contemporary woman in a perfectionistic death trap from which many will never escape, for no woman can find happiness when she is addicted to perfection either in herself or in others. Contemporary women, supported by their mothers, the media, feminism, and their own grandiosity, have come to have such high expectations of life and of others that they are no longer able or willing to make the compromises necessary in love. Marion Woodman argues that modern woman is "addicted to perfection,"[5] seized by her power drive and her need to control and dominate. It is interesting to note that Woodman's analysands were high-achieving career women suffering from food disorders, usually bulimia or anorexia; food was often the only way in which these women could experience any deep intensity of feeling. In addition, everything in these women's lives had to be perfect, their bodies, their work, their men, their clothing.

"SETTLING": DOING THE BEST YOU CAN

But life, alas, is not perfect, and neither are men. In earlier times, women simply "did the best they could" when it came to finding their hero. They held up the institution of marriage itself as a meaningful pursuit, and thoughtfully and realistically chose the worthiest suitors as their husbands. There were even jokes about going to college to get your "MRS." But no matter how humorous one made the nature of the pursuit, it was a meaningful and an *essential* one. As in any career, if one couldn't get the presidency, one settled for the vice presidency or a lesser station.

Women did the best they could and yes, they did *settle*.

"Settle," of course, is a word that nobody likes to use today. But settle these women did. They understood and accepted life's limitations. They had an innate sense of their biological clocks. They knew the value of a good man to their future and the future of their children. They accepted and accommodated their own needs to mother and to bond. It has been argued that these women had an *overly* strong sense of bonding, and there is some truth to this observation. Nonetheless, this acceptance of and belief in the feminine role allowed them to realistically evaluate their options and choose a husband—hopefully a good one.

BEING THE RIGHT PERSON

But finding a hero and bonding in the way in which our mothers did is difficult for the contemporary woman. She is not only perfectionistic, overstriven, and grandiose about herself and others, she is also the victim of several delusional systems of which she must divest herself before she can proceed with her life.

The first is her quest for a Ghostly Lover, the perfect male who does not exist. The second is her belief in "Big Lie Number Nine: The Myth of Self-Sufficiency," a belief to which she clings tenaciously in spite of indications from her unconscious that she has other needs. These indications may come in the form of anxiety and panic attacks, psychosomatic symptoms, restlessness, insomnia, eating disorders, and compulsive overwork.

One cannot quite so easily undo that which has been done, and many a modern woman who professes her wish to wed simply doesn't know where to begin. This is indeed a complex undertaking, an internal as well as external journey; one cannot find a hero until one makes some changes within oneself. Perhaps this is why my father always used to say that "finding the right person is much more a question of *being* the right person."

A "GOOD MAN"

Where, then, does one begin? Believe it or not, one begins with the Madonna aspect of the personality, the part of womankind that has suffered a crisis through the last wave of feminism and the sexual revolution. Women who are in the process of embracing their femininity, as outlined in Chapter Five, may already have some sense of how it is that the Madonna aspect is helpful in overcoming Ghostly Lover problems, for it is the Madonna which gives a woman her values, patience, and perspective. And it is the Madonna which makes ordinary men into heroes.

The Madonna in a woman knows what a "Good Man" is and appreciates and values him. Because this aspect of female personality sees the best in *everyone*, the woman utilizing her Madonna is able to see the very best in a man. The Blemish game is thus also avoided, for the woman connected to her Madonna is looking for strong points, not faults. Superficial flaws and imperfections are easily overlooked; the Madonna aspect of personality is deeply spiritual and is responding to the man in terms of his value as a life partner, not a weekend paramour. This, however, is no small feat for the Amazon-Courtesan type, who is used to selecting her men in terms of their ability to stimulate and play with her. Once, I told my mother that what I really needed was a man who made me laugh. She said, "If you want to laugh, get a feather and go tickle yourself."

This was the attitude of the old Mother-Madonna: Marriage was not a laughing matter. Marriage was serious business, one to which a woman devoted herself. If a woman is truly in search of her hero, her Madonna must wait patiently and respond discriminately while her Amazon leads and lights the way. It is the Amazon within the woman which motivates her to socialize in the proper environment; it is the Madonna who intuitively knows a Good Man from a bad one. The Madonna, it must be remembered, is the center of the soul, the center of the woman's own goodness, courage, and integrity, the part of her that is in touch with her deepest values.

SHARED VALUES

But the modern woman is deeply confused about her values and is always looking for a man who "shares her interests." In *Married People*, Francine Klagsbrun found that shared interests were not particularly important to an enduring marriage, but shared values were.[6] Of course, just because couples don't share interests doesn't mean that they don't do things together. Paul Newman and Joanne Woodward, for example, do not on the surface have a lot in common. But he goes to the ballet to satisfy her interest, and she goes to the auto races to satisfy his. They share in each other's activities not so much because they are interested but because they share the value of mutual support.

Robert Johnson, in his study of romantic love entitled *We,*[7] points out that initial romantic infatuation is nothing more than the projection of one's anima or animus values onto another. Something in the appearance or the personality "captures" the ideal notion of male and female in the other. Over time, this fantasy ideal gives way to reality; the couple get to know one another and perceive the "real" person behind the projected ideal. This is when romantic love or infatuation fades, and true love is tested.

The man and the woman are now challenged to "take back" or "own" their projections or expectations of the other person and accept that person as he or she really is. It is here where shared life values, goals, and attitudes come strongly into play, for this is the "glue" of which relationships are made.

Many of us have watched the enduring love relationships of our own parents, who were more likely than the current generation to base their union on the sharing of values rather than romantic infatuation. My own parents, married close to fifty years, are markedly different each from the other, so much so that one wonders at first how they have survived together all these years. She is fastidiously neat, he disorderly; she Victorian in manner and attitude, he just "one of the boys." Nevertheless, their shared life values, sprituality, ethics, and commitment to each other have sustained them throughout the years.

"A Better Man Than She Is"

But it was more than this. What really has sustained them through the years is that Mother has always viewed him as her hero, a Good Man worthy of her respect and devotion.

What, then, is a Good Man, a man one can view as a hero? A Good Man is dependable, committed, considerate, loyal, hardworking, protective, and respected by other men in his field. Most of all, he has courage and integrity. Upon hearing this description, a colleague of mine laughingly suggested that this man sounded something like a Boy Scout; indeed, in his youth, he may well have been. A woman does not choose a Good Man—her hero—in quite the same way as she would choose a good lover or playmate. A Good Man, in fact, often does *not* make a good playmate, and may even at times seem—well—just a little bit boring. Yet this tendency toward predictability is a key sign that the gentleman in question may indeed be a Good Man, a man a woman can count on, a *better man than she is*.

"A better man," quite simply, is a man who has strengths and attributes which the woman can admire and respect, attributes which in some way allow her to yield a certain amount of personal control to him, for she knows that this man—the man she is to view as her hero—is trustworthy and dependable. Without this trust in him, it is impossible to relinquish any control whatsoever, and the woman continues to function in the male role. When with a man she can trust, however, the woman is then able to relax into her femininity, cheerfully relinquish some of her control, and enjoy some of the pleasures of being a woman.

In short, then, a man who is a hero is a trustworthy man to whom a woman feels she can safely surrender and with whom she feels some sense of personal completion.

This is an extremely important part of choosing one's hero, for later on in life the woman may find herself in one of the most dependent positions she will ever encounter, that of pregnancy and childbirth. Here, as at no other time of her existence, she will be at the mercy of nature and will need the support and the protection of the person nearest and dearest to her, her husband. But the groundwork for this intense and intimate relationship must be laid long before marriage. It begins with the woman's decision to trust and lean upon the man, not because she is incapable of caring for herself, but because she has decided to join her life and her body to another. Since one can never escape being the gender which one is, the woman must always deal with the fact that she is a woman and will need to lean on her man and on others through the very natural yet inhibiting times of childbearing. As Sylvia Hewlett points out in *A Lesser Life,* the demands upon a woman's time and her body by childbearing and child-rearing have been largely ignored by the feminist movement,[8] so much so that women today have truly forgotten the protective role of the men in their lives during these demanding periods.

TRUST TAKES TIME

But the need for a hero in a woman's life goes well beyond her need for a protector in childbirth and thereafter. No, the need for a hero is deeper and stronger than that, for if men cannot be heroes to women, then women are forced to be heroes unto themselves; this, as we have seen, is a deadening and dreary business. Women are best able to live out their feminine aspects when they give over some of their male dominance to the opposite sex freely and unconditionally. When a woman is willing to do this, she inspires enormous confidence in her man and enhances not only his masculinity, but her own femininity as well.

The *choice* of a man is extremely critical, for love is often blind and even foolishly unconditional. Even extreme Amazon Women seem to slip unconsciously into a feminine modality when deeply in love; they often adapt to the whims and caprices of even an inadequate man. The *I Ching* states "In yielding, there is strength," but this is true only if one is yielding to a trustworthy person.

But how does one know if it is safe to trust a man? Trust takes time; it has to grow. It is foolhardy to believe one can trust a person instantly, though many men and women may boast that they "know" a trustworthy person when they see one. Women, notoriously romantic creatures, have a dangerous way of trusting a man based only on sexual and romantic arousal, perhaps because it is too difficult for them to engage in sex without at least the illusion of trust. I call this "inventing love," something many women feel they must do in order to allow the invasion and penetration of their bodies so quickly in a relationship.

In reality, trust can only be established over time, as the man proves that he will be there for the woman across a wide variety of situations and life experiences. A man who is to be a hero to a woman will allow her the opportunity to lay down her Amazon armor piece by piece. A woman is foolish to take it off all at once and stand defenseless before a man who may not, when tested, prove trustworthy.

Often a woman is surprised to find her hero in "the boy next door," a man she has known a long time, perhaps a man who has stayed in the background of her life, highly magnetized to her, always interested in her. She may not find such a man to be as thrilling as newer, less familiar prospects. She may not even wish to consider him as her mate. But one thing is for certain: She can trust him.

"I didn't used to think S. was as much fun as the other men in my life (he'd been through the party scene and was sick of it), but he's one of few men I've known I can completely trust and depend upon. He *never* lets me down," said one Amazon Woman who had spent the last ten years searching for her hero, when, in fact, he was waiting for her "in the wings." "We have quarrelled and even stopped speaking to each other, yet he's never abandoned me. He waited a long time to have sex with me, and after sex, his tenderness and caring grew stronger. We have been through a myriad of life experiences together, we understand each other, and, if I need him, he's only a phone call away.

"I realize now that S. loved me deeply for many years in a simple, uncomplicated way. He knows me well—including my faults and problems—and he still accepts me. But years ago, when he first told me that he loved me and wanted to be with me always, I dismissed it as idle talk. I just didn't seem able to

believe him. I guess I wasn't ready for a Good Man.
I was looking for excitement, for trouble. I wish I
knew then what I know now.''

Why Do I Always Want
the Ones Who Don't Want Me?

Groucho Marx is credited with having said, ''I
wouldn't want to be a member of any club that
wanted me.'' This is consistent with Marion Woodman's observation that the contemporary Amazon
Woman suffers from a highly inflated ego on the one
hand (grandiosity) and extremely low self-esteem on
the other.[9] Psychologically, it could certainly be speculated that the former is a compensation for the
latter. Beneath the contemporary woman's grandiosity often lurks a secret fear of being less of a woman
and a real difficulty with accepting love when it
actually happens for her. But perhaps we all, male
and female, question our own self-worth; it is common, it seems, to question the good judgment of
someone who deeply loves and cares for us, for we
know and understand our dark side or ''shadow'' in a
way which no one else can. And because we know
our own inadequacies so fully, it is easy to dismiss
someone who truly loves us as a fool.

So many women over the years have asked me this
plaintive question, ''Why do I always want the ones
that don't want me?'' What about the ones who *do*
want you? Almost invariably there is a Good Man
like S. somewhere hovering around a woman's life,
forever magnetized to her, thinking that she is wonderful. But the woman's grandiosity, her Ghostly

Lover, and her fear of intimacy and entrapment all combine to sabotage any possibility of making such a man a hero.

MAGNETIZING MEN

Which brings us to perhaps the most essential thing about finding one's hero: It is best to select from among the men who are *magnetized* to you. Simply put, this means that he finds you, you do not find him. Magnetic energy is arousing. It radiates from a woman's feminine center, "pulling" a man toward her. Dynamic energy, by contrast, is goal-oriented and aggressive. A dynamic woman may catch the man she pursues but often fails to maintain a magnetic hold on him.

It has already been pointed out that the contemporary woman is what Jung and his followers would call "animus-possessed," i.e., seized by the masculine aspects of her personality to the exclusion of the feminine. Since Jung identified masculinity as "knowing what one wants and doing what is necessary to achieve it,"[10] one can see that the animus-possessed Amazon Woman is highly goal-directed and dynamic. Thus, if she desires marriage, her tendency will be to go after it with the same directness and fervor with which she pursues her other life goals in the impersonal world.

With the dynamic approach, a woman may indeed "catch" a man, but the man she catches may often be of a less aggressive and more feminine type, or simply too immature and vague to assert himself and escape. As for the more masculine men she pursues, most of them will not initially reject the sexual or maternal overtures which the aggressive woman might make, for what man would not, for a time, enjoy a woman's easy sexual availability and nurturing? Sadly, the woman who is dynamic and aggressive in her personal life often finds herself "catering to a man" in a way which would make any radical feminist shudder, while reaping none of the long-term rewards which should follow from such a high investment of self.

An excellent example of the misuse of one's femininity and poor selection of a hero can be found in the case of G.G., a hair stylist who doggedly pursued a prominent client of hers in spite of the fact that this man had shown no interest in her outside of their professional relationship. Nonetheless, she decided that he was "the man" for her, invited him over for dinner, then continued to "court" him, calling him often, cooking for him, sending him cards and gifts, giving him free haircuts and back rubs, and eventually having sex with him. Deeply disappointed and confused when he did not return her calls or her affections, G. could not understand that she had been pursuing a man without having any indication of *his* attraction to *her*.

An Amazon Woman such as G. must accept the fact that no matter how dynamic she is in the external world, it is important for her personal fulfillment to be magnetic, not dynamic, in her relationships with men, for only then can she be assured of the man's attraction to and desire for her. If she insists on remaining dynamic in her personal relations, she forces herself to keep working, once again "doing" as opposed to just "being." The aggressive and independent woman who chases men often deeply and secretly longs to be swept away by a more powerful modern-day Theseus, but instead, her dynamic intensity often clashes with theirs and repels them. On a practical level, this usually means: Don't call him; let him call you.

The Amazon Woman must learn to do that which has come to feel most alien to her: She must learn to just *let it be* and select her hero from among those men whom she magnetizes and inspires from the start.

TAKING INVENTORY

The modern Amazon Woman needs to "take inventory" of herself and her life, objectively evaluating the reality of her situation. The process of "taking inventory" should be done as objectively and honestly as possible: What do I really have to offer a man, what is the competition, and whom have I attracted so far? These questions can be difficult for the contemporary woman to answer, for her tendency is to structure things as she thinks they should be, as they ought to be, rather than accepting them as they simply are. It is important that a woman in this position attempt to look clearly at the Good Men she has thrown away, and why. It is not unusual to find women well over thirty who have never received a proposal of marriage from a man, either because no man was so inspired or because the woman herself did not allow any relationship to grow to this level of intimacy. Such a woman must examine objectively the men who are characteristically attracted to her, not vice versa, for these are the men who are most eligible for a committed relationship.

And, as pointed out earlier, these men will *not* meet one's Ghostly Lover expectations; that is, there will be some way in which they will be flawed. Each woman must decide for herself the flaws she can live with in her hero. Chronic unemployment and physical abuse, for example, are problems that are usually insurmountable; other flaws (odd personality traits, physical imperfections, unusual personal habits) can perhaps be more easily overlooked.

FINDING YOUR MISSING PART

Finding one's hero can be likened to finding one's "missing part," the aspect of personality required for one's completion. In *Knowing Woman,* Irene Claremont de Castillejo writes, "Love happens. It is a miracle that happens by grace."[11] The miracle of which she speaks is that sense of completion which we feel, that wholeness as we merge with our invisible partners, the missing parts of ourselves that we may find in union with the opposite sex. This "chemistry" takes many forms, but there seems to be some truth to the adage "opposites attract"; extremely feminine women often attract extremely masculine men, and sensitive men are often attracted to strong and thinking women.

It has long been observed that in this type of partnering, the man and the woman involved often start to take on some of the characteristics of the other, that is, they start to exchange each other's traits. P., my country musician friend, a man who is almost all sensation and diffuse awareness, used to say to me: "You make me *think* about things."

Whereas I would say to him, "And around you, I *feel*." Maybe that's the magic of love.

The contemporary argument, of course, is that one is supposed to find one's completion in oneself, not in another, and to some extent, this is true. But this is a process that must occur over a lifetime. Marriage is the ideal environment in which to realize this process, especially if one's marital partner has some of the attributes which one lacks and to which one can aspire. While some individuals do succeed in finding their completion on their own, most men and women develop more fully through a loving relationship with another human being. Ultimately, it is only through love, through finding our missing parts in another person, that we are transformed.

How do we tell when we have met a partner who represents our "missing part"? Mostly it is a feeling, a sense of comfort and wholeness deep within the self. As a broad generalization, however, it might be stated that the performance-oriented woman is more apt to require a sensation- or feeling-oriented man. Stated somewhat differently, the more "focused consciousness" a woman projects during the day, the more "diffuse awareness" she requires in her man at night. A woman who is severely tilted toward her Amazon, seized by a "calling" or career of some substance, will often require that her "missing part" be a man of a sensitive nature, a man of serenity, patience, compassion, and understanding, so that she may experience a sense of completion and peace in her life. Interestingly enough, these are the very characteristics which men traditionally have enjoyed in their Mother-Madonna wives.

This does not mean that the strong Amazon Woman

need choose an inadequate man as her hero. On the contrary, such a woman's "invisible partner"[12] can certainly be what I am calling a Good Man, perhaps someone in a creative or helping profession, such as a writer, teacher, artist, or doctor. This sort of man often possesses the patience and compassion that the Amazon lacks; he has the power to heal the warrior woman's wounds. But even here, where the Amazon aspect remains prevalent in the personal relationship, the woman may find she still cannot optimally relate to her man unless she embraces her femininity and is willing to view him as her hero. No matter how kind and gentle her man, he wants to be viewed as a hero *by her*.

DANCING AT TWO WEDDINGS

The woman who is dominant in the external world may not find this easy, for, like a man, her tendency is to bring her dominance in the marketplace back into the home. Slipping gracefully into one's femininity, embracing one's Madonna and Courtesan can be difficult (at times impossible) after a hard day's work. Little wonder that so many women are giving up on the fantasy of "having it all." Many women today are deciding quite simply that they would rather have love and are quietly checking out of the marketplace; yet others continue the delicate balancing act between two kinds of consciousness, two different ways of being in the world and relating to men.

My mother always used to say, "You can't dance at two weddings." In fact you can, sometimes even with some success but usually with a great deal of stress and at tremendous cost. As indicated earlier, more than 50 percent of the most successful female executives in this country have remained single while another large percentage of those who have married remained childless, and today, as never before, contemporary American women are looking closely at the costs involved as they live out the masculine side of their nature to the detriment of the feminine.

IT IS RUMORED . . .

Many contemporary Amazon Women have discovered that they take a secret pleasure in dominance by men, for they have learned what every sadomasochistic aficionado will know: Submission can be downright relaxing. Perhaps this is why the great diva Maria Callas is reputed to have engaged in violent arguments and even fistfights with the fiery Aristotle Onassis. Perhaps there is something in all women which yearns to be subdued and conquered, and the advantages of such a surrender will be explored further in Chapter Eight. But even the enlightened Amazon Woman, the woman who truly wishes to embrace her femininity and surrender to a man, has a difficult task ahead of her, for there are few Actual Men available.

Modern movements have created a generation of hard women and soft men, men who are easily controlled by women. It is the poetic, gentle, and "soft" man who is willing to tolerate and "understand" the Amazon Woman; tough Actual Men don't want the job. The contemporary soft man comes in various forms and guises. At his weakest, he's called "the wimp." On a criminal level, he's a character-disordered sociopath. On a developmental level, he's a "Puer

Aeternis," an "eternal boy" not yet grown to man-hood. This latter type of adolescent male was de-scribed in detail by noted Jungian analyst Marie-Louise Von Franz in her classic study *Puer Aeternis*.[13]

THE PUER AETERNIS: AN ETERNAL BOY

Von Franz tells us that the term "Puer Aeternis" is first found in Ovid's *Metamorphosis*, where he refers to a "child god of antiquity, a divine youth who is also a redeemer."[14] The literal translation from the Latin of the term "puer aeternis" is "eter-nal boy," and Von Franz uses the term to describe a type of man who is fixated in adolescence.

At the time Von Franz delivered her "Puer" lec-tures (1959–1960), this was a fairly uncommon char-acter disorder, although she did comment that "the problem" was becoming quite pronounced even then, along with a marked increase in homosexuality. To-day, twenty-five years later, it would be safe to say that the Puer Aeternis is your average young man. Popular psychology has referred to him as a "Peter Pan," a boy who won't grow up. This syndrome has been popularized most recently by Dan Kiley in his best seller *The Peter Pan Syndrome*.[15]

My own references to the Puer Aeternis on the radio have elicited an extremely strong response. I was amused to receive a letter from a gentleman asking the name of Von Franz's book, which I had recommended on the air. His wife had said it de-scribed him perfectly, but she couldn't remember the title. "Something like the 'Pooh Bear Eternal,' " he wrote. Unwittingly, this man had translated the cumbersome Latin of Von Franz's term into the easily identifiable cuddlebear we all know and love.

The Puer *is* a "Pooh Bear"; he is warm and playful—almost "magical." He can always make a woman laugh, even despite herself. He desires all the pleasures of love, but is not willing to endure the difficulties of loving. He is symbiotically bonded to his mother, not yet his own man. In general, he views most women as mothers and is particularly spoiled sexually, having had all his sexual needs met by mothering women. He is forever looking for the perfect mother figure (one with whom he can also have sex) and is perpetually disappointed because all he can find are women who have needs of their own.

"I don't know what to do about my boyfriend," said one of my Amazon Woman callers, a thirty-five-year-old successful businesswoman who had been living unmarried—in *her* condo—with the man in question for four years. "He's a wonderful friend and lover. We have terrific times together, but he can't seem to get his career on track, and he says that he can't make a real commitment to me until he does. I don't mind paying more than my share of the bills; I just wish he could find himself. He's a composer, a real creative genius, but there just isn't a market for his kind of avant-garde music. I try to encourage him to try composing more commercial material, but he says he doesn't want to compromise his artistic integrity. It's not that he doesn't want to work. It's just that he hasn't quite found his professional niche. He did take a straight job selling stereo equipment, but he hated it and didn't last more than three weeks. Then he tried to start his own recording studio, but that never got off the ground, and he lost the five thousand dollars that I lent him to get it going. So now he's a chauffeur for a limo service. But that's not really *him*. He's so bright and talented. I just wish he could realize his potential."

The Puer lives in the Land of Potential, the unreal world of pipedreams and promises. He has great difficulty with accepting the harsh realities of life—with commitments of any type—for he is not psychologically well grounded. He often takes a job that's "not really him" until the "right thing" comes along. The trouble is, of course, that nothing ever seems to feel "quite right," not his work or his relationship or his life. Like the adolescent, he is still testing the waters, checking out the options, hoping for a break, waiting to grow up, suspending his actual life. Eric Berne described this life pattern as a "when" script (life will really begin *when* . . . I'm thirty, I'm forty, I get the right job, I meet the right woman, etc.). If we consider a "life script" to be a representation of the ongoing drama of existence, the "when" script dictates that life is not taking place in the present, but will happen sometime in the future.

Much like the Amazon Woman, the Puer's sense of unreality stems from a fear of being trapped, bound to any person or situation. And indeed it is the same mothers who raised Amazon Women who brought up Puer Aeternis men. More often than not, these adolescent males are the Amazons' brothers and lovers. Just as the Amazon avoids reality by working constantly, her Puer comrade-in-arms often avoids reality by *not* working. Both are fixated in adolescence; she afraid of bonding and marriage, he afraid of commitment and growing into manhood. Both parties feel what Susan Littwin calls a "sense of entitlement,''[16] a narcissistic belief that the world owes them a living and that they deserve care and support from the other without giving anything of themselves in exchange. Both are self-centered and wish to be taken care of, but neither wants to—or often even knows how to—take care of the other. Thus, there are many contemporary Puer-Amazon relationships wherein two very needy, self-involved people are feeling cheated and uncared-for.

This is not to say that an Amazon Woman should not choose a Puer-type man as her hero, especially since there are so many of them (and they have, after all, been created by women). Even a so-called "eternal boy" *can* grow into manhood, especially if he is inspired by a woman who understands and cares about him. To inspire her Puer to the heroism he is capable of achieving, a woman may have to suppress some of her mothering instincts. She must be cautious not to be overly solicitous of him, for then he remains a little boy, not a man. This is difficult, especially for the Amazon-Mother type of woman, who may feel an irresistible urge to preach and teach. Such a woman must allow her Puer man to make his own mistakes, to grow into manhood, and, ultimately, to protect her.

BAD BOYS

Unlike the Puer, the nature of the sociopath is such that he cannot be "raised." The word "sociopath" was first coined by Hervey Cleckley, who brilliantly analyzed and described this character disorder in his classic study *The Mask of Sanity*.[17] The sociopath is a kind of Puer Aeternis, but he is not a good boy; he is a bad boy. Unlike the Puer, who has simply not grown up, the sociopath has a total or partial lack of conscience, depending upon the severity of the disorder.

At its extreme, we are talking here about the criminal mind, which is characterized by what Freud called "lacunae" in the superego, that is, "holes" in the moral structure. Such a man is more than just immature; he is manipulative, devious, and dissociated from the needs and feelings of others. Nonetheless, he is enchanting to many women, charismatic, highly articulate, energetic, exciting, attractive, and amusing. The devoted women in his life are used at his whim as toys for his own pleasure. Although sexually active, the sociopath is capable of divorcing sexuality from true intimacy. He is loved by women, but disappoints them repeatedly and fails to show appropriate remorse.

Amazon Women, longing for immediate gratification and hungry for excitement and dominance from men, are often attracted to these disturbed individuals. The bravado, derring-do, and colorful pasts of sociopathic men often make them *appear* to be heroic. On the contrary, they are dangerous to almost any woman, and hardly "hero material."

From Clark Kent to Superman

Far preferable as a potential hero would be the much-maligned so-called "wimp," the Good Man beaten down, divested of his masculinity. Within every meek and mild-mannered Clark Kent there lives a Superman which a truly inspirational woman can bring out. To give such men back a sense of self, and *not* fall prey to the almost irresistible urge to continue the castration, is a challenge which should be undertaken with care. Any woman can beat a man down; few are capable of truly building him up.

With the exception of the sociopath, these varieties of "soft men," while perhaps not conforming to the modern woman's idealized version of a hero, represent viable options for her, especially since the "Actual Man" is in short supply. Many Actual Men are already married, others are much older. And a large number of age-appropriate mature males around have been negatively affected by the feminist wave; they've become spoiled, aggressive, angry, arrogant, and at odds with women. Many an Actual Man, having stood tall through feminism, has a sense of fighting women for his life. He retaliates defensively, often approaching a woman with an arrogance that's really saying,"I'm the man around here. You're not a better man than I am. If you think you are, prove it." Often, he just wants to have casual sex with her, after which he discards her. Every time this happens the man feels victorious and the woman is defeated, reaffirming what women secretly suspect: Sex for men can be nothing. Yet it always feels like something to a woman.

SEX: THE BIG DIFFERENCE

Today's woman is, for the most part, freed from her sexual repressions; the question of the day is, free to do what? Many women find themselves in live-in relationships which have no future; yet others become sexually involved long before they feel emotionally ready. Today's woman gives her body freely, perhaps more freely than any other woman in history, yet asks and expects little in return in the way of commitment. This leaves her feeling empty and unfulfilled; in spite of the sexual revolution and feminism, the sexual act appears to have remained for women a far more significant encounter than it is for men, and this, again, gets back to "Big Lie Number Five: The Myth of Sexual Sameness."

Sex is an undeniably intense experience for both genders, but it is intense in two extremely different ways. For men, sex without love is a simple physical release. This is rarely true for women. Even the most perfunctory sexual act seems to carry emotional significance for women, so much so that they are often astonished when they find that the man does not share their feelings. While sex seems to intensify loving feelings in women, the same cannot be said of men. Sometimes, in fact, the sexual act can devalue a woman in a man's eyes, toppling the woman from the pedestal and dissociating him from his ability to see the Madonna aspect of her personality.

Many otherwise sensitive men have candidly shared with me their experience of the sexual act devoid of love, often comparing it to a basic bodily function such as excretion. The male sexual drive seems to have an aggressive and primitive aspect to it that is rarely found in women. Orgasm for a woman is an opening up; in man, it is a spewing forth. This aggressive male sexual instinct is tempered greatly by the power of love; that is, by the man's caring for the woman. This, in fact, is what slows men down and turns them into good lovers. Sexually sophisticated women are certainly familiar with the profound difference between the man who is inspired to make love as opposed to the one who merely wants to have sex; uninspired by loving tendencies, the average man can easily ejaculate in less than a minute. Most contemporary men, however, make some attempt at lovemaking regardless of their feelings for the woman, for today's sexually sophisticated woman will not tolerate anything less. So even here, one cannot be truly certain of what is going on; lovemaking can certainly take place without any real love existing.

When, then, should a woman have sex with a man? If she is *not* interested in a committed relationship, the answer is: Anytime she wishes. But, on the whole, today's woman is tired of casual sex and is truly wanting to effect a commitment with the hero of her choice. Given that she has found her missing part, her invisible partner—her hero—how does she know when to give him her body?

"What Are Your Intentions, Sir?"

This is a difficult question for, as we have discussed, women tend to read much more meaning into sexual relationships than actually exists. One thing, however, is certain: *Time* is the critical factor here. It is only with time that a man can truly get to know a woman and fall in love with her. Exactly how *much* time should pass before a particular woman should have sex is impossible to say, but if the woman is interested in marriage, she should look for signs of "honorable intention" in a man.

In olden days, a woman would simply inquire, "What are your intentions with me, sir?" This question, which used to be considered a woman's *right* to ask, now strikes terror, not just in the hearts of men, but in the hearts of women as well, who fear that they will alienate the gentleman at hand. It is important, therefore, that the woman state tactfully but clearly what she is wanting of life and a relationship with a man—not in the form of an ultimatum with *this* particular man—but in the form of a general statement about her desires, e.g., "I'm basically a one-man woman," "Sex is a very special expression of love for me," or "Casual sex is so meaningless." These statements don't leave a man feeling like you're dropping a net over him but do give him an idea of the kind of relationship you're looking for. Making such statements—and even having men agree with them—does not guarantee that a relationship will be permanent, but it does represent a good beginning, helping to prevent much pain and confusion later on.

Take, for example, the story of V., a young woman who was sexually involved with a physician for a period of ten months. While they had exchanged many words of affection, he had never, in fact, stated his intention to be monogamous nor had she directly asked for it. Toward the end of their relationship, when V. discovered her physician with another woman, she was flabbergasted. He simply said to her, "I never promised you anything, did I?" And indeed, he hadn't: The expectation of monogamy was *hers*, not his.

Until a reasonable amount of time has passed, most men will be unable to state their intentions with a woman. But the wise woman will wait until she is comfortable that some degree of love *precedes* sex, and that his intentions are consistent with hers.

PREMATURE SEXUALITY

R. telephoned my program to say that she had met the man of her dreams and wanted to know how and when to get him to make a commitment to her. "He loves me," she said. "I just can't get him to talk about marriage." She told me that the two of them, next-door neighbors, had been seeing each other almost constantly for six months. When I asked how soon after they'd met had they started to have sex, she giggled nervously and replied, "After two weeks." Then she hastened to repeat that the gentleman loved her very much and they had grown very close together. "How do you know he loves you?" I asked. "Does he tell you that?" No, she said, he didn't "exactly" tell her; she just knew. "*How* do you know?" I repeated. R. was quite obviously disturbed by my question; she stuttered and started and corrected herself several times, unable to come up with much more than that she knew he loved her because of the way *she* felt around *him*.

In truth, she had very little real information about his feelings. All she knew for sure was that he spent large amounts of time with her—most of it devoted to sexual play. No wonder she was having trouble talking about marriage to this man! He was apparently in the relationship simply for the fun and convenience of sex-next-door. Since he'd never said or done anything to express feelings of genuine love and care for her, there should have been no logical reason to believe that he felt them.

But R. was not being logical. Having given her body—and a part of her soul—to this man, she was caught in the sweet but powerful grip of Eros, the principle of love, not Logos, the principle of logic. Woman in general is dominated so completely by Eros that often when she has sex, she feels the power of that love so strongly that she is certain that the man must also be in love. As such, she is consistently disappointed when he doesn't wish to commit himself to the casual relationship that she fervently believes holds profound meaning for both of them. So common is this phenomenon that many women today have decided in favor of celibacy before a marital commitment is made. They have recognized that for most women, the ultimate commitment is sex; for most men, it is marriage.

"TREACHEROUS WHORE!"

Premature sexuality, however, is but one of the pitfalls in finding a hero. Of equal danger in terms of undermining an evolving committed relationship are the Amazon Woman's friends, the modern "Moon Maidens of Artemis." Contemporary single Amazon Women tend to band together in order to give each other the support they are not receiving from men. They often encourage each other's relationships with Puers and sociopaths—even going so far as to share them—because these men do not threaten Amazon friendships. Yet once an Amazon Woman finds a man she can consider to be her hero, her Amazon girlfriends may well retaliate against her. Inadequate but lovable men are tolerable; heroes are not.

Armed with their Scythian swords, these modern Moon Maidens of Artemis will shoot arrows into any worthy man, finding his "blemish" like expert archers. They do this out of fear of losing their comrade-in-arms. In addition, her bonding with a man contrasts sharply with their own chronic loneliness and isolation. These "sisters" may sabotage and even do great damage to her relationship in much the same way that Hippolyta's Amazon Moon Maidens never forgave her for bonding with Theseus. Eventually they killed her, one of them shouting "Treacherous whore!" as she shot an arrow through Hippolyta's heart.

Such "friendly" attempts at sabotage are only a few of the many obstacles that lie in the path of a woman's surrender to her hero and to her own femininity. The great myths and fairy tales often show the young woman being forced to endure great trial and tribulation before she is allowed the bliss of union with her hero. The quest for a hero is a lonely voyage, likely to be undermined, not supported, by friends and family, who often see the successful woman as "selling out," i.e., underestimating her own worth, when all she has really done is come to terms with reality.

And coming to terms with reality is the antidote to grandiosity and the Ghostly Lover, for, in a very real sense, they are one and the same. Grandiosity is an inflation of the self; the Ghostly Lover is an inflation of a man. When one takes a more realistic view of oneself, one can then take a more realistic view of men in general. The possibility of real relationship and love between man and woman then begins to exist with all its pain and pleasures, glories and imperfections.

"Taking a Chance on Love"

The Amazon Woman, having embraced her femininity and divested herself of her grandiosity and her Ghostly Lover, is now ready to deal with the world of reality, and this means that she must learn to take love where she finds it and be receptive to its possibilities. She does not pursue men but responds appropriately to those who pursue her, as she feels comfortable. She is magnetic, not dynamic, for dynamism is for warfare, magnetism for love. The dynamic capabilities of the woman, however, must certainly be used in allowing her to socialize properly; even the most feminine and magnetic woman must call upon her Amazon aspect to "get out of the house" and mingle with eligible men in any way which interests her. She may wish to join a church, synagogue, or special-interest group, making herself available and visible to men who share her values.

Whichever route a woman takes to be visible to men and attract them to her, it is important that she then make reasonable judgments about the men who are actually in her life, as opposed to her fantasy projections. M. Esther Harding makes this point when she discusses the ways in which women are apt to be pulled away from reality by their Ghostly Lovers, sometimes preferring the beauty and the enormity of the dream to the mundane concerns of daily life. Such women, she says, are foolhardy, for "surely it is better to catch a little fish and land it than to hook a great fish and be pulled under the water."[18] Many a modern woman has been lost to her dreams and ideals, pulled away from reality by visions of life and relationships which were philosophically appealing but psychologically untenable.

It is as much a crime against nature to be too rational as it is to be too capricious, and many a modern woman has discarded a Good Man in favor of a good job because her unrelated animus was not checking in with her deepest feelings. Well over a decade ago, Jungian analyst Irene Claremont de Castillejo queried, "Has woman's libido gone so far over to the masculine world of ideas and mechanics that the feminine passionate concern with life is actually denuded of the libido which it needs in order to hold the balance between the opposites?"[19] In fostering her feminine side, modern woman is challenged to take risks once again, this time in the world of love, not in the world of power. These risks are even more difficult than before, for the modern woman has much to lose and often is not clear as to how much she might gain. "Taking a chance on love" is riskier than ever these days; the contemporary woman is no longer innocent, naive, trusting, or unsophisticated, yet she must be willing and able to be all of these things in order to love in the deepest sense.

The Amazon Woman who has embraced her femininity and found her hero still has much unexplored terrain before her. Like Hippolyta, she may still be slightly dazed and frightened. And like the great Amazon queen, the modern woman may soon discover that she has much to learn about the fine art of managing her newfound hero, the subject of our next chapter.

CHAPTER SEVEN

Managing Men: Handling Your Hero and Making Him Yours

No modern woman would dream of undertaking a new project or business without understanding something of the nature of the product or service involved. Yet many a modern woman attempts to embark upon a relationship with her newfound hero without so much as the slightest idea as to what male psychology is all about. Magnetizing a man is one thing; holding onto him is quite another. Many a man who has cheerfully "taken the bait" soon loses interest after just a few nibbles, and many a woman who calls my program reports to me that she has difficulty sustaining a relationship. Often these women think it is enough to give a man time and sex; they understand little about the true power of their femininity and even less about men.

However much contemporary Amazon Women attempt to embrace femininity, many will continue to buy into "Big Lie Number Two: Androgyny"; that is, they will persist relating to the opposite sex as if men and women were psychologically the same. There are, of course, differences among men. The argument has already been made, however, for the desirability of what has been called the Actual

Man, and this chapter will, in fact, be devoted to the understanding and management of the mature male.

CASTRATION ANXIETY

The first thing that must be understood about men is that their greatest and most primitive fear is that of castration, both physically and psychologically. Men fear the hook and, even more, the net. Psychologically, this is known as "castration anxiety," and no woman can hope to understand and manage men without awareness of this very primitive and basic male fear.

The physical fear is obvious; men are indeed more vulnerable, more exposed, more directly aware of both the power and fragility of their sexuality. A woman's sexual organs are protected and hidden, a secret even to herself unless she goes to the trouble of actually looking, mirror in hand. A man, by contrast, can always tell what's going on "down there," often much to his chagrin. While a woman's most common sexual problem has to do with orgasm, men's sexual concerns center around penis size, potency, and staying power.

Castration anxiety appears to be present in all men to one degree or another, sometimes revealing itself in frightening dreams or fantasies. Few men consciously fear the literal cutting off of their genitals. But all men seem to contain within them the psychologically analogous fear of consumption by women. And indeed, in every act of intercourse, the man *is* consumed, if only for a moment. The woman may be penetrated, but it is the man who is *swallowed*. Man's

primitive fear of the vagina and of women in general
is as old as history itself, manifesting itself across
cultures in myths and in legends which have common
themes and visual images, caves and razor-sharp teeth
being the most prominent.

Men are afraid of women, and with good reason.
A man in love is "not himself"; he has, at least for a
moment (and perhaps for a lifetime), lost himself to
another, and this threatens his sense of freedom and
autonomy. A fish, like a man, wants to swim free.
He has a natural attraction to the bait but an aversion
to the hook. This aversion to entrapment is profound:
It is represented in fairy tales as being eaten by the
witch (Hansel and Gretel), swallowed by a whale
(Jonah), seduced by the sirens (Ulysses), and sucked
dry by the Harpy and the Harridan. Castration fear
can be found in every culture. The overbearing American woman is nicknamed a "ballbreaker"; in Latin
cultures, she is called "La Brujita," the little witch,
a crazed, desperate, barren woman who preys on
unsuspecting men.

It is ironic that literally all research studies indicate
that the large majority of men flourish within a successful marriage. They live longer, enjoy better health,
and generally report a higher level of well-being.
Nonetheless, men do resist domesticity; they are hunt-
ers by nature, and their natural instinct is to run free.
As has been discussed in earlier chapters, a man's
psychological individuation and journey into manhood are largely contingent upon his successful separation from his mother, the first woman in his life.

In early childhood, a young boy is indeed symbiotically bonded to his mother, appropriately so. But if
he remains owned by her into adulthood, he can

never be free to give himself to another woman or experience the full power of his manhood in the world. Freud wrote at great length about the young boy's pre-Oedipal fantasies of sexual union with the mother, fantasies which must be repressed and redirected if the boy is to grow to maturity successfully.

PRIDE AND PERVERSITY

The mature male, then, has developed himself and worked hard psychologically to ensure his separation from mother, and will not readily risk being consumed by another woman again soon. The highly masculine man often seems characterized by an emotional rigidity which is not easily penetrated, especially in the first half of his life. Often he seems unduly proud and overly defended, much to the woman's distress. Since women do not suffer castration anxiety or share the man's developmental history, it is difficult for them to understand this typically male attitude.

Yet understand it they must, for these castration fears operate at deep levels of the unconscious mind. The contemporary woman's insistence upon sexual satisfaction, strength, sensitivity, and tenderness from her man does not seem unreasonable, yet in the words of Christopher Lasch, "rational arguments notoriously falter in the face of unconscious anxieties."[1] Even the most enlightened man seems to harbor an unconscious aversion to the "liberated woman," for she calls up in him primitive fears "of a possessive, suffocating, devouring, and castrating mother," according to Lasch.

It can be astonishing for the unenlightened woman

to learn the high levels of reassurance and special handling which even the most powerful and seemingly adequate mature men require. It has been customary among modern-day feminists to suggest that such men are "immature," whereas in reality they are merely men, and behaving as such. Boys will be boys; there is no getting away from it. American women have been deceived into believing that behaviors typical of the mature and actualized man are regressive and pathological in nature, whereas these behaviors are, in fact, nothing more than normal attempts at maintaining a sense of integrity and manhood.

The woman who does not understand male pride can simply never understand men. Men are overly proud (by comparison with women) principally because they suffer castration anxiety and fear losing their manhood to women. *The woman's task, then, is to reduce this fear and show the man, in a myriad of ways, that she will not castrate him but will enrich his life, light the way, and enhance his masculinity.*

Much has been written about the "frail male ego" in the last two decades (as if writing about it would somehow render it less frail), and modern woman has railed against the notion of supporting her man. Yet the rewards of this support can be enormous, both for the man and for the woman. The man who is admired by his woman is inspired to live up to her conception of him, and her positive belief in him is greatly rewarded by his increased tenderness and love for her. More to the point, however, is that any other attitude on the woman's part simply *does not work* for the relationship. The critical or castrating woman reaps only the bitter fruits of indifference from her man, either making him less than he is or forcing him into a position of withdrawal or rebellion.

Recently, a thirty-four-year-old woman called my radio program to complain about her unsatisfactory relationship with her fiancé, a factory worker. She was in banking and moved in a world in which he did not feel comfortable. He refused to attend the company functions, and this was becoming a source of great dissension between them. I inquired as to whether she in turn attended the parties and social gatherings at the factory. She stuttered and stammered and finally confessed that she did not.

It soon became clear that her man (whom she claimed to love dearly) was merely defending his manhood. He would not move into her territory unless she showed some willingness to move into his. In rebellion, he was finally turning to other women, who were undoubtedly more supportive of his position in life than was his executive bride-to-be. The amazing thing was that this obviously intelligent and accomplished woman could not understand why she had failed to obtain the fidelity and interest of a man she professed to love.

ACCEPT HIM AS YOU FIND HIM

No woman can hold a man if she fails to accept him as she finds him. Yet many women lose the men they love, men who genuinely love them, simply because they secretly believe that they can change them. Men, of course, do change, but not because women want them to. They change when they are ready and motivated. Over a period of years, the banker might have found that her factory worker lover gained a higher degree of comfort among her executive-level friends; under pressure, however, he could only feel inadequate. And it is quite possible, in this instance, that the woman did indeed find her lover inadequate, and he sensed this and resented it. While this example may be extreme, it is nonetheless illustrative of how foolish women can be in their attempts to change the men they love.

Accepting a person as you find him goes far beyond simple tolerance; tolerance implies that you are aware of his many faults, but that, being a good, kind person, you are choosing to overlook them. Accepting a man as you find him, at face value, making the decision to look up to him as your hero means truly embracing the entire man *as he is*. It means feeling deep within your heart and soul that he is totally acceptable to you. It is from this place that real loving begins.

This acceptance of a man at face value is one of the most difficult aspects of a continuing and successful relationship, for almost all women feel compelled to try to change the man of their dreams, however perfect he may seem initially. And these efforts are seldom, if ever, met with success. For men are not only proud, they are *perverse* as well; that is, the more a woman tries to tell a man to do something, the more likely he is not to do it!

And why are men perverse? Because they unconsciously fear castration. A man once said to me, "I cannot be told by a woman; I must be persuaded." He did not understand why; he only knew that it was so. Another man put it this way, "Do you know how to get a man to marry you? Don't want him to."

Both of these men were making a strong, though

unconscious, statement about their natural male perversity. Men resist being ordered about, not because they genuinely wish to dominate women (although this may certainly be true of some men) but because they subconsciously fear losing control, which is tantamount to losing their manhood. In reality, these very men relinquish a great deal of control to the woman who supports their manhood; with her, they no longer feel threatened.

How, then, does one go about supporting and nurturing a man in a personal relationship? Clearly, one must work out of a basic understanding of male psychology, an understanding which revolves around castration anxiety, pride, and perversity. In addition, however, it must be remembered that in spite of his defensive mechanisms, a man still needs the love, kindness, compassion, and sexuality that the right woman can bring to him. So how to proceed?

As outlined in Chapter Five, femininity is best embraced through the Madonna and Courtesan aspects of personality, with the intelligent bright light of the Amazon leading and guiding the way. The Amazon aspect initiates the process of "reeling him in," for before a woman can truly exercise her feminine powers, she must first pay close attention to her man and his *specific needs*. And here, often, is where the Mother aspect of femininity comes into play, along with the woman's Madonna and Courtesan. Some men require a great deal of mothering, others spiritual or inspirational guidance, and yet others a high level of sexual excitation.

But even here there are subtle differences which must be observed; mothering to one man may be smothering to the next, playful sexual invitations to one may be wanton behavior to another. The rules of love are never easy to write, and the very attempt may justifiably be viewed as outrageous. The rules of love, in fact, are not rules at all, for love is intuitive, visceral, and spiral. Its very essence is its mystery, and one loses much of its magic when one tries to define that which ultimately can never be defined. Yet the attempt, however prosaic, must still be made. Each woman can use the following examples and illustrations as guidelines in her own feminine process and development.

MOTHER, DON'T SMOTHER

Let us start, then, with the maternal aspect of femininity, an extremely powerful aspect of personality which can be used for good or ill in relation to man. It is the part of a woman that nurtures and supports a man, encouraging him to grow and actualize himself and realize his greatest potential. Like the Amazon, however, the Mother also has a dangerous tendency to cut down and castrate. The classic shrewish wife is acting out of the negative side of her Mother aspect; she criticizes, henpecks and demeans her husband, forever keeping him a frightened, insecure little boy.

When mothering is overdone and inappropriate, it becomes *smothering*. This is when men feel overwhelmed, swallowed up, consumed by a woman. Often it is the Madonna aspect that intuits a man's need for nurturing and the Mother that fulfills it. If the Mother aspect operates too independently of her Madonna and her Amazon, a woman will often overdo mothering and give too much.

Excessive mothering is of no benefit to men, to children, or to women themselves. Here, more than in any other aspect of femininity, judgment must be exercised. Excessive mothering was particularly prevalent in the fifties; this is, in part, what feminists were responding to when they renounced the maternal aspect of femininity as "catering to men." A classic "reaction formation" then occurred. "Reaction formation" is a psychoanalytic term referring to a syndrome which occurs when, in an effort to correct a particular problem, one swings all the way to the other extreme. For example, a very shy person trying to overcome his shyness will often suffer a reaction formation and become obnoxiously overbearing. The sexually inhibited woman will sometimes, in an effort to compensate for her inhibitions, become promiscuous. So it has been with the maternal aspect of female personality; the fifties woman was excessive in her mothering, while the eighties woman, in a classic reaction formation, is deficient.

The contemporary woman often fails to grasp or appreciate the power and significance of her Mother aspect with regard to men, although the yearning to bear children does not seem to have diminished significantly. Frequently, maternal warmth toward and care of men is viewed as demeaning rather than fulfilling, and, as a result, today's woman is often viewed by men as cold and lacking in nurturance. Little wonder that so many women succeed in attracting men, yet fail to hold them. In typical Amazon fashion, they have exalted what is between their legs and discarded what is deep within their hearts. As discussed in Chapter One under "Big Lie Number Six: The Denial of Maternity," many contemporary women have rejected the maternal role and then wonder why they fail to be compelling to men as women.

I once asked a man what sorts of things he wanted a woman to ask him to make him feel loved. To my surprise, the first thing he said was, "Are you hungry?" The next thing he said was, "Are you tired?" He went on to say that when asked "Are you hungry?" he didn't necessarily expect the woman to run into the kitchen and prepare a huge meal. He might be just as willing to take her out to dinner. What he liked was that the question was being asked.

The maternal woman need not appear to herself or to others as beaten-down or subservient in any way. Rather, such a woman, at her best, is a source of comfort and refuge, a place to which a man wishes to return no matter how painful his stresses in the outside world or how low his self-esteem. In *Women and Sometimes Men*, Florida Scott-Maxwell states, "One of the poignant paradoxes in the life of a woman is that when a man comes to her, he so often comes to recover his simple humanity and to rest from being at his best. So a woman frequently has to forego his better side, taking it frequently on trust as a matter of hearsay, and she accepts his lesser side as her usual experience of him. . . . She longs to see his greatness but has to meet the claim of his smallness."[2]

It is during these times that the Mother aspect of womanhood is most severely tested, for men often come to their women tired, weary, irritable, coarse. Even a great man needs a place to be small, and the place where all men look to do this is at home with their women. Women who fail to accept this role vis-à-vis men seldom sustain an enduring and loving relationship.

Even heroes have their weaknesses, their "Achilles' heels." According to the *Iliad* of Homer, Achilles was the greatest of Greek heroes. He obtained his phenomenal strength from being immersed in sacred waters by his mother. However, the one place where his mother held him as she dipped him into the water, his heel, was the single part of him where he was not invincible. The myth of Achilles is symbolic of the fact that the man's bond to the mother is what makes him forever vulnerable to and needful of women. Woman may need man's protection, but man's need of woman is equally great.

Every man has an Achilles' heel. It may be alcohol, food, stress, or social discomfort. Some men are sensitive about being short, fat, or bald; others about their upbringing or education. Whatever the man's Achilles' heel, the Amazon's tendency is to draw her sword and go straight for the jugular, to criticize and castrate wherever she senses weakness. But if she plugs into her Mother aspect, her loving capabilities will take over and she will actually shield her man from his own inadequacies, helping him, but in such a way that first and foremost preserves his dignity.

The other night, I had dinner with J., a full-blown, very macho Actual Man who has a weight problem. My Amazon couldn't help but notice he has very poor, self-destructive eating habits. If there was something unhealthy to eat on the menu, he ordered it, fatty foods over light, starches over greens, meat over fish. Before I had embraced femininity, I would have told him directly, "Don't you know that all that fatty red meat and greasy fried potatoes are bad for you?'' Having embraced femininity and learned how to be more maternal towards men in a less aggressive way, I simply modeled some appropriate eating behaviors and, through indirection, got him to share my dinner.

I started with a fresh green salad, took a bite, and said, ''Oh, this is wonderful—so delicately done!'' J. reached over to my plate and took a forkful. Seizing the moment, I nonchalantly placed a few spoonfuls of salad on a nearby bread and butter dish, and said, ''This is much too much for me; why don't you just pick at it?'' Which he did. Then my seafood arrived (as did his New York steak and fried potatoes), and we repeated the performance. I noticed his real pleasure in my ''feeding him''; my subtle nurturance was being well received. I made no judgments about his food as opposed to mine, never referred to caloric content or nutritional value. I simply shared my food with love. Because it was loving, not overwhelming, he was receptive and appreciative.

Another appropriate way to exercise the maternal aspect of personality with a man is when he is physically ill. At these times, a woman may be extremely solicitous and nurturing without danger or fear of smothering him. This is a good time to pay close attention to a man's needs; during illness, individuals tend to become regressive, childlike, and demanding. Some men will request certain foods, usually associated with childhood; others will simply want to sit and talk; and still others may wish to be left alone.

All men have mothers, but they have experienced different mothers and different kinds of mothering. Some men require a great deal of nurturing, others do not. The secret is discovering the level of mothering

to which a man is most receptive. Even men who
have been smothered by their mothers still require
some mothering from the women in their lives, but
that mothering must often be indirect and very gentle. Other men have been severely deprived of nurturing and need a great deal. The bottom line is *sensitivity*
to another person's particular needs and requirements.
Most mature or Actual Men, always defending their
sense of strength and adequacy, find it very difficult
to admit any weakness or neediness. Like the most
American of heroes, the astronauts, they're made of
"the right stuff" and deeply appreciate a woman's
tenderness when something has gone wrong with
their "equipment."

"How can I think of their needs when I have so
many of my own?" asks one of my distressed callers. "*I* am hungry. *I* am tired. *I* am stressed-out. I
want them to make these inquiries of me. I guess
what I want is mothering from my men."

Modern women are so masculine in their orientation that they *often* look for mothers in their men.[3]
Then they are bitterly disappointed in the men whom
they ultimately attract, because the fact is that they
are also wanting *men* in their men. Feminism led
contemporary women to believe that they could have
it all (Big Lie Number One). But just as women
cannot have it all or *be* it all at one time, neither can
men.

Sensitive, nurturing, maternal men have difficulty
expressing aggression and drive. Conversely, the hard-
driving, hard-achieving Actual Man has difficulty
expressing caring and tenderness. This is why he is
especially needful of maternal nurturing from women.
The harder the man is on the outside, the softer he is

on the inside. The more fully realized the man (the more responsible, powerful, and protective he is), the more mothering he usually will require from the woman in his life.

The Mother aspect of personality is best expressed through a genuine caring for and commitment to the well-being of another. It often works in tandem with the Madonna, for much intuition is required in knowing when to move forward and when to back off. Hippolyta, though hardly a hausfrau, was adept at this. Theseus remarked that while she was a constant source of support to him, she also had the facility of almost disappearing into thin air when she sensed her presence was no longer required. Once, during an embarrassing confrontation with a baron from Athens, Theseus recalled, "I turned to speak to her, but she was gone without my hearing a footfall. So it was then and often after. If she thought herself a hindrance to me, she would be off like a deer in covert. She would come back as quietly, saying nothing of it from love and pride."[4] This is true caring and sensitivity, utilizing both Mother and Madonna aspects of the feminine personality. These behaviors establish an enduring and almost unbreakable bond between a man and a woman.

THE IDEAL RELATIONSHIP

At this point it might be well to stop for a moment and consider what, from a psychological point of view, constitutes an ideal relationship between a man and a woman. As discussed earlier, the personality of each human being can be seen, in transactional analysis terms, as containing three parts which Eric Berne called "ego states": the Parent, the Adult, and the Child.[5]

The Parent part of the person contains the attitudes and values, the Adult is the center of thinking, and the Child is the center of feeling and sexuality. It is the Parent part that instructs, teaches, evaluates, nurtures, and criticizes. It is the Adult part that makes decisions, tests reality, and intellectualizes, and the Child part that is playful, spontaneous, and sexual.

Both men and women contain these three ego states within their personality in one degree or another. Some people are top-heavy (too much Parent), others are bottom-heavy (too much Child), and yet others, bulging in the middle, are overly rational and intellectual (too much Adult). Whatever the personality type, however, a successful relationship between a man and a woman depends upon having smooth and noncrossed transactions between her Parent, Adult, and Child, and his.

For example, if the Parent within the woman attempts to relate lovingly to the Child within the man, and he is receptive and responds appropriately, this is a clean transaction. But if the woman attempts to mother the man when the man is not in the mood for mothering, he will respond not with his Child, but with his Adult or perhaps even with his angry Parent. This is a crossed transaction and usually reflects a lack of sensitivity on the woman's part; that is, she has not utilized her intuition (her Madonna) to tune into her man's needs.

In an effort to integrate the Jungian and Bernian concepts, I would venture to suggest that the Parent is analogous to the Mother, the Adult analogous to the Amazon, and the Child analogous to the Courtesan in the female personality. The Madonna is a bit more complex (the Madonna always is) but can be conceptualized in transactional analysis terms as residing in a thinking part of the Child commonly referred to as the "Little Professor."

There is no question but that intuition or the Madonna is central to deciding which ego state to utilize in a woman's interactions with a man. If she chooses a dynamic aspect, such as the Mother or the Parent, and the man is not in a receptive mood, she is in trouble. If, on the other hand, he is in a playful or sexual mood, coming out of his Child, and she has not yet melted her Amazon armor so as to get into her Courtesan or Child state, she is also in trouble. Sensitivity as to where the other person "is" psychologically is central to the success of all human relationships. Because of her heightened intuition, the woman often seems more adept than the man at sensing the emotional and feeling tone of the other. Ideally, the woman "knows" (with her Madonna) exactly when to use her Parent (Mother), Adult (Amazon), and Child (Courtesan) with her chosen man.

Clearly, there is no one way to act with any one given man. But it can safely be said that all men require all four aspects of womanhood at some time or another. The woman's ability to shift ego states appropriately will in large part determine the success of her relationships. The remainder of this chapter will not attempt in any way to encompass the many situations in which a woman may find herself with a man, but rather will attempt to highlight some of the areas in which modern woman is most deficient.

THE BLACK MADONNA

The contemporary woman's Crisis in the Madonna, the inspirational or idealistic aspect of woman, has already been discussed. But it must also be said that there is a dark side, the Black Madonna, a cold aspect of womanhood which must withdraw from a man when he has "done her wrong." No man loves or respects a "doormat," and it is a foolish woman who does not act appropriately when a man has behaved badly or disappointed her.

Anger and disappointment are usually best expressed through the Black Madonna's silent withdrawal, although a spirited kind of feistiness can be effective as well. This is very different from direct confrontation, an aggressive cutting down of the man which is castrating and only forces him to fight back. Silent withdrawal gives him time to think and reflect upon his wrongdoing; feistiness makes him admire the woman's courage and spunk. The latter is best accomplished through direct and childlike expression of feelings (remember, all feeling comes from the Child within the person). An example would be, "I feel hurt, used, disappointed, furious, sad, etc." Incredulousness is also useful ("I can't believe that you would do this!") and also brings the Madonna into play.

TEARS AND LAUGHTER

Tears and indeed any other emotional and spontaneous expression of feeling can be seen as a part of the Courtesan aspect of personality. Tears should not be feigned, but should never be avoided if they come naturally, for tears are an honest expression of pain and hurt and can sometimes speak louder and more forcefully than words. This dispels the myth of "Big Lie Number Seven: To Be 'Feminine' Is to Be Weak," for nothing is more compelling or engaging in a woman than an authentic expression of her deepest feminine feelings.

One reformed Amazon Woman put it this way: "I always know that I feel deeply about a man when I am able to cry around him. I need to be so tough on the job. Tears are simply not allowed. This carries over, of course, to my personal life. I've been controlling my tears for so many years that I'd almost forgotten how to cry. I *know* my Amazon armor has been melted when I can let the tears flow freely. At first, I felt really stupid, crying in front of a man. It made me feel weak and defenseless. Then I realized in some way I was actually stronger for it. Oddly enough, it was always good and never bad. Men felt more protective around me. It almost always caused them to stop fighting with me, and I felt greatly unburdened and relieved of my pain."

It might be recalled that it was only when Hippolyta finally cried that she was able to release herself from her impulse to kill Theseus. In many ways, her weeping could be seen as the turning point in their relationship, the point at which she decided to embrace her femininity and renounce her warrior ways.

Even more powerful than tears, however, is the Courtesan's lightness and laughter. The spontaneous expression of joy and sexuality are delightful to mature men for Actual Men often have a kind of grim seriousness about them, a by-product of the stresses and pressures they experience in the working world.

Modern Amazon Women, unfortunately, tend to have the same stresses. Nonetheless, unless one wants to spend one's time with Puers, sociopaths, and wimps, it is often the *woman* who must diffuse the seriousness of the man with her teasing playfulness, sexuality, and flirtation. Again, as with mothering, many contemporary women will object to this Courtesan role; under the spell of Big Lie Number Seven, they think of it as being in some way demeaning, rather than seeing it as a feminine power which can be utilized to greatly enhance one's life and one's relationships.

It might be well to remember Noel Coward, famous for having said he had nothing more than a "talent to amuse." The modern woman would do well to develop hers. Contemporary Amazon Women are, by and large, stimulating, but often they are not very amusing. They are intense, challenging, difficult; often they just make men tired.

"Lighten up," smell the flowers, sing, dance, laugh at his jokes, and tell him stories. Remember Scheherazade, who saved her life and kept her king by spinning a different tale every one of a thousand and one nights. Sexually, it is most important to be responsive. As one man so succinctly put it, "Enthusiasm counts for a lot." This makes perfect sense when one recalls man's fundamental castration anxiety and need for reassurance sexually and otherwise; the responsive woman confirms his adequacy and masculinity.

"I went with a man for a full six months before I really had an orgasm with him," said L., a sexually "liberated" but personally unfulfilled young businesswoman. "For once in my life, I did not complain or tell him how to be a better lover. Actually the problem was mostly mine. I wasn't used to being with an Actual Man, and he scared me half to death. I decided to just enjoy it as much as I could and communicate that pleasure to him. Each time we made love, he said to me, 'I love it when you're excited like this' or something to that effect, and he always seemed eager to make love to me, which is more than my ex-husband used to do. Fortunately, he never actually asked me if I came, so I really didn't have to fake it or lie about it. I *was* experiencing some real pleasure; I just wasn't quite getting over that edge. Well, each time we made love, I kept positively reinforcing him just the way you told us to, guiding him gently this way or that way, moving a little bit to better ensure my pleasure, and finally, I just started having orgasms all over the place. It's hard to put this into words, but I can say this: I know that my enthusiastic response to him set a positive tone for our relationship and allowed me finally to really get it together.''

Many men and women who call my radio program complain that they simply have no desire to continue lovemaking due to the lack of enthusiastic response on the part of their partners. Clearly, no man or woman wishes to engage in the sexual act unless he or she feels desirable and desired by the other.

SHOW HIM THAT YOU NEED HIM

Similarly, no man will wish to continue a relationship with a woman when he does not genuinely and sincerely feel *needed* by her. This is poorly understood by most modern women, who have fought long and hard for their independence. Because this self-sufficiency is an attractive aspect of personality to *them*, they assume it will be equally attractive to men, especially since so many men pay lip service to this, claiming to admire it. But admiration is different from love or caring; the independent woman often inspires admiration but not devotion. *"Show him that you need him,"* I tell my lonely Amazon patients, and they respond, "But I do! I do!"

Contemporary women *do* need men; they have just forgotten how to communicate this. Often they feel embarrassed to ask for help even when they are ill or hurting emotionally. They fix their own cars and leaky faucets, travel alone, pay their own bills, and wield their own credit cards. Little wonder the average man feels superfluous in their lives and often gravitates to the less adequate woman, who seems to need him. Yet underneath the Amazon armor, I frequently discover just a frightened little girl yearning to be taken care of. "How can I show a man I need him when I make a six-figure income, drive an expensive sports car, own my own home, and am sending my children through boarding school?"

Note here that this woman has defined herself in terms of what she does and has, not in terms of what she *is*. This brings us back to "Big Lie Number Eight: Doing Is Better Than Being," i.e., activity is better than passivity. If this woman and others like her would be willing to just *be* with a man, allowing him to care for her in the best way he knows how, appreciating his maleness and genuinely communicating that appreciation, she would soon get from men the protection she so fervently craves.

Today's woman only *seems* independent; emotionally, she often emerges as more needy, insecure, lonely, and desperate than her mother and grandmother before her. Refusing to nurture men, she in turn has not been nurtured by them; refusing to be tender with men, she has not been tenderly treated by them. Her aggressive independence has given men nothing to protect, so she has not been protected. Behind the Amazon armor often lives a terrified woman less sure of her place in the world than ever before. Filled with the rhetoric of egalitarianism, these women have discovered how unfulfilling relating ''man to man'' can really be.

Relating to a man as a woman means allowing oneself to feel soft once again, surrendering to a strength which is uniquely male and permitting oneself to feel pleasure from it. This is the true significance behind the seemingly trivial daily acts of life which men and women traditionally share: opening doors, helping with coats, leading the way, arranging the evening. Many women today actually feel a sense of shame in the feelings of girlish dependency which these small acts engender in them. Others simply feel foolish. They have concluded that simply because they are *capable* of doing something for themselves, they *ought* to.

Such an overstriven and independent attitude in women engenders a feeling of impotence in men; men who feel impotent often react in angry and unpredictable ways. Feeling useless, they often lash out in rage or withdraw completely. Men cannot bear children or propagate the race; much of their sense of adequacy and importance comes from their protective function vis-à-vis women and children. In order to foster better male-female relationships, women today must decide to allow men to do that which is most natural to them. In this way, women will be able to retrieve much of that which they have lost while still retaining most of what they have gained. First, however, they must understand the quintessential differences between the male and the female.

Down through history, tales have been told of man and his quests—for the Holy Grail, for the Golden Fleece, for the head of a fire-breathing dragon. Invariably there is a fair maiden involved, and she, too, is relentlessly pursued until captured. In twentieth-century America, this all has a somewhat archaic ring to it, yet the male's need to be challenged and prevail remains. Perhaps no one likes that which is too easily won, but the male of the species seems to have a particular disdain for it. This is why the hard-to-get woman is so often alluring, and why men so easily lose interest in the woman who is "easy."

REEL HIM IN SLOWLY

Be patient. Men fall in love in the spaces; that is, when they are away from a woman and feel her absence. Don't be afraid to let a man go if he wishes to. Every good fisherman knows that pulling too tautly on a line will often snap the rod and pull the fisherman down too. A good woman is one who is secure in her femininity and knows its power. And when she has no power with a particular man, she soon knows that too, and gracefully lets go. Paradoxically, today's seemingly strong women are incredibly deficient in this respect, painfully and pathetically holding on when it is clear to all but themselves that they wield no feminine power. It is here—in the agonizing and fruitless relationships which so many women endure—that the desperation and neediness of today's woman really manifest themselves.

Living together, in particular, has been anathema to the contemporary woman's search for commitment. Few women find a long-term living-together arrangement satisfactory, and fewer still are willing to bear children under these circumstances. Living with a man is tantamount to overfeeding the fish but never quite getting him on the line. Such fish merely get glutted and bored. Similarly, in living-together arrangements, men get what they want—Mother, Madonna, and Courtesan—but women do not get what they want—male protection via commitment and marriage. That this remains a primitive need in women is to me indisputable. More women call me with the problem of uncommitted intimacy than any other. It is not enough merely to father a child; most women wish that a man would "husband" it as well. Note here that the word "husband" is used as a verb and not a noun, a word of action, meaning "to manage prudently and economically." While many women today do not give nearly enough of themselves to men, others give too much of themselves, expecting nothing in return. Tough and smart, savvy and sexy, these women have learned how to negotiate for everything but a commitment.

KEEP HIM WANTING

How then can a woman best maintain a high interest level in a man, one sufficient to lead to an enduring commitment? While there are no surefire formulas, it is extremely important for a woman to understand the power and validity of a concept in psychology known as "partial reinforcement."

Psychologists specializing in learning theory have discovered that behavior is best reinforced when rewarded on a variable and intermittent partial reinforcement schedule. This means that a woman should reward a man with her company and sexuality some of the time (but not all of the time) in unpredictable ways. Men who are rewarded and nurtured constantly, as in live-in relationships, are not as motivated to commit to a woman as men who are not. Live-in lovers lose their motivation; in psychological terms, they are easily subject to "satiation" or boredom. Partial and unexpected reward or reinforcement, however, keeps a man in a state of high expectation and arousal.

Many a woman has observed the ease with which she receives commitment from a man in whom she is not really interested. Why is this? Because the woman "keeps him wanting," exposing him to the power of partial reinforcement. When a woman is relatively indifferent to a man who is pursuing her, she naturally and easily "hangs back" a bit. This rewards the man unpredictably, only a *part* of the time. Suppose, for example, a woman has had two dates with a man, but refuses him a third time. Upon his fourth invitation, however, she might find herself alone on a Saturday night (perhaps abandoned by her favorite man of the hour) and may yield to her new suitor's advances. He then feels victorious and encouraged; he may have struck out once, but feels he got a home run on the first, second, and fourth swings. *This* is partial reinforcement. The man is excited, encouraged, yet challenged; his attentions have been well rewarded, though somewhat unpredictably. This arouses his passions even further, and he will pursue the woman with even more energy than before, provided he remains magnetized to her and the time they do spend together continues to be pleasurable and rewarding.

Unfortunately, women fail to behave this way with men with whom they wish to get serious. When excited about a man, the Amazon Woman's tendency is to "jump right in" and give him everything all at once. Remembering from Chapter Six what a perfunctory act sex can be for a man, this is foolhardy. Even more importantly, however, the lack of partial reinforcement will tend to quickly satiate the man and reduce the probability of forming a continuing attachment leading to a commitment.

Many a woman wonders how she can gain a marital commitment from a man who is reluctant to "get serious," even though they have been seeing each other exclusively for several months. My "prescription" is almost always: "See other men. You must go out—if not with other romantic suitors, then at least with platonic male friends." But often a woman with a commitment problem protests she is not interested in seeing other men; she wishes to spend time only with the man she loves. Without him, she experiences "separation anxiety"; that is, she feels as if a part of her is missing. And these feelings are quite normal. Nonetheless, a woman must be willing to endure the pain of separation in order to test the relationship and the depth of the man's attachment to her. For femininity does *not* mean that a woman abdicates control of her personal destiny. While it is important to be attentive to a man's needs, a woman must never ignore her own. She must use the strong and intelligent Amazon aspect of her personality to protect herself, to maintain her independence, and to stay "in circulation," until such a time as her man clearly demonstrates his loyalty and commitment to her.

The concept of partial reinforcement can thus be summarized as follows: Be available, especially in the beginning, when attachment patterns are forming and excitement is at its highest. Then *vary* your availability slightly, allowing him time to miss your company and suspect you are in the presence of other men. *Be* in the presence of other men during these intervals; it will enhance your feelings of self-esteem and desirability. Keeping options open in this way prevents a woman from feeling desperate and overly dependent upon one man, until such a time that her special man is ready to make a commitment. These benign but effective tactics are also useful in keeping the pressure off relationships; men, it must be remembered, do not like the feeling of being hunted and trapped.

Psychological principles of partial reinforcement can easily be applied to a love relationship as long as the woman remembers to remain magnetic and not dynamic, allowing the man to pursue her and rewarding him frequently, but not to the point of satiation.

But this is not all. The remaining element which will heighten the possibility of commitment in a relationship is a far less scientific concept which can only be called "feminine mystery."

FEMININE MYSTERY

J. is an example of a young woman who failed to understand the power of feminine mystery. She called my radio program complaining about her loneliness and isolation, claiming that she really didn't trust men and didn't know how to "get close" to them. When asked what she meant by this, she explained that her relationships would be just fine until the man invariably said that she was "too uptight" and asked her to "open up." With trembling and trepidation, she would proceed to do just that. She opened up, "spilling her guts," revealing all her secret fears and needs, only to find that the man would flee in terror.

When I was a little girl, there lived down the street from us an old Polish woman named Mrs. Girecki. She and my mother exchanged a lot of old folk wisdom, and one of the things Mrs. Girecki told my mother was "Only show a man half your ass." In more elegant terms, this is what's known as feminine mystery.

Now that modern woman has tasted masculine power and its rewards, she is once again hungry to discover her feminine potentialities. Hopefully, she can learn that femininity, too, is powerful; magnetic, mesmerizing, artful, and, at its best, irresistible. To throw away such power is foolhardy; any man in possession of such a weapon would use it to its fullest capabilities.

Social and cultural changes have occurred and continue to occur, but the need of man for woman and woman for man is unchanging; I have attempted to communicate only the basics of this in this chapter. Each woman must figure out for herself how to be changeable and mysterious, exciting and alluring, intellectually stimulating and spiritually inspiring. All men are different, and yet all men are essentially the same. They all want, each in his own way, Mother and Madonna, angel and whore, all in one woman. No one woman can be all things to all men (though some women come close), but the constant discovery of how to continually engage and excite a man you have already magnetized is one of the most challenging and fascinating aspects of being a woman.

But the best is yet to come. For much of the magic of relationship is found in the woman's willingness to surrender to the hero of her choice, the subject of our next chapter.

CHAPTER EIGHT

Sweet Surrender:
Body and Soul

"The fight is over, Hippolyta, and you are not dead. Will you keep your vow?"[1]

So said King Theseus to the half-stunned Amazon Queen as he pinned her to the ground they battled upon. Her "vow" was an oath of surrender: If the Athenian King won their contest, as he did, Hippolyta had sworn before all the Moon Maidens of Artemis to take him for king and follow him.[2]

Hippolyta's eyes searched the sky, as if looking for guidance. But no sign appeared, no heavenly command, no word except for the rude mutterings of the Athenian warriors and the anxious whispers of her Moon Maidens. Finally, the dazed queen sat up, as if from a dream, and spoke. "So be it," she said, and Theseus gathered her up, his strong arms under her knees and her head resting upon his kingly shoulder. She lay quietly in his arms "as if they had been made for her, feeling her fate and her home."[3]

This is *it:* the ultimate female fantasy of being "taken," transported, ravished, "swept away," carried over the threshold of love in the arms of a valiant hero. It is a theme of countless books and movies, perhaps the most popular of which is that spectacular scene in *Gone with the Wind* where Rhett carries Scarlett up the stairs. The sight of the gargantuan brute King Kong scooping up delicate little Fay Wray in his huge hairy paw is anther great cinematic vision of *ravishment*.

RAPE AND RAVISHMENT

What, exactly, is ravishment, and why does it inspire such high levels of excitement in almost all women? This chapter shall attempt to answer these questions, for ravishment can only occur when a woman surrenders herself to the power of love, both within and without.

Ravishment must be distinguished from rape, for rape is an act of violence; ravishment, an act of love. In both acts, a woman is seized and carried off, but here the similarity ends. When raped, a woman is taken by an enemy through brutal sexual assault. When ravished, a woman is taken by a lover to ecstasy and rapture. Obviously, ravishment cannot take place without the woman's consent, i.e., without the woman's surrender to the man.

Surrender. The very word conjures up visions of defeat, of shame, of submission. Yet in love, as opposed to war, surrender is sweet, for it enables the woman to fulfill her deepest feminine potentialities, both sexually and emotionally.

Mind, body, and spirit are involved in this process, and although there are strong unconscious forces always at work in affairs of the heart, the modern woman will find that it is her conscious ego which will offer her the most resistance and must be valiantly fought. The unrelated animus of the Amazon Woman is an ever-present danger to the process of surrender, throwing up his sword at every turn, raging and thrusting and resisting the natural flow. Only an extremely well-centered woman, a woman with a strong sense of personal identity, is ready to begin the process of surrender, and it is assumed that women about to embark upon this journey have a strong enough ego to deal with the profound feelings and emotions which will burst forth.

Becoming a truly receptive woman, a woman oriented toward love rather than power, can be a frightening and at times overwhelming task. This transformation is often experienced as a complete disintegration of the personality, a kind of falling apart. Long after she had surrendered to Theseus, Hippolyta recalled:

"When you threw me and got my sword, that was a death to me. I woke all empty . . . I thought, 'Now I am nothing.' "[4]

Yet from that "nothing" grew a new sense of something, a birth, a renewal, a new kind of power which is born of love.

LOSING TO WIN

When a woman relinquishes some sense of her ego to a man, she, in fact, gives up her resistance to him, and allows him to penetrate both her body and her soul. She is indeed, in some sense, "conquered," for she has yielded both emotionally and physically, yet she has also been "victorious" in that she has allowed nothing to stand in the way of union between her and her man.

It is my hope that by the end of this chapter, the modern woman will see that surrender in love can only be a triumph. Yielding to the right man, the hero of one's choice, ties the bonds of the relationship even tighter. One might again recall the wisdom of the ancient Chinese saying from the *I Ching,* "In yielding, there is strength." In making this statement, the great Taoist masters were, in fact, acknowledging the tremendous power of receptive femininity. Many practitioners of the martial arts say that this receptive potency arises from the breath; in the Orient, this is called "Chi" or "Ki," the "breath of fire." Through yielding with the breath, a martial arts master, however slight of build, can easily conquer a muscular opponent twice his size. Similarly, woman conquers man, but only through her receptivity, her yielding to him in the name of love.

Why is this necessary? Because it is in the nature of things, of life itself. Women need to do it to feel truly alive; men need to experience it to feel adequate as men.

BEING RIGHT OR BEING LOVED

Years ago, a man I loved told me that we were never going to make it together. "Each of us is always going to want fifty-one percent," he said. We argued. Finally, in frustration, he said, "You just don't understand men."

Time has passed. I have come to understand men better, their universal castration anxiety, their pride, their perversity, their urgent and primitive need for that 2 percent, that illusion of control. And often I have wondered, as the years have passed, what it would have meant had I relinquished that 2 percent gracefully.

Let us get on with it, then. The remainder of this chapter shall be devoted to pragmatic and concrete ways to facilitate the process of surrender, but it must always be remembered that a *loving attitude* is at the heart of it all, for without this, no surrender can take place. This brings us to the first issue at hand, namely the choice of *being right versus being loved*.

Men need to be right, even when they are wrong, and smart women know this, and let them. Male perversity and stubbornness are less of a mystery when one fully grasps the concept of castration anxiety; still, the initial frustration of yielding to male willfulness can try the patience of even the most Madonna-like woman. Yet the alternatives to surrender in trivial matters are even more taxing: arguing, bickering, sarcasm, withholding of affection. Since it is usually the woman who is more in touch with the feeling tone of the relationship, it is most often she who must elect to lay down her weapons in the name of love and declare peace. One of my listeners, A., wrote a letter in which she expressed her triumph in surrender in this way:

"Why surrender? The only other option is to continue the fight. When we are sick and tired of being sick and tired, we will surrender.

"How I surrendered: I had to lay down the weapons (my mouth, dirty looks, hostile body language, etc.) and I quit defending my right to be right. I had to surrender to win. I won peace, serenity, respect.

"When we surrender, we allow other people to be

exactly as they are and we no longer have to be hero, victim, or martyr. We are free to be exactly who we are (wife, mother, student, employee, or whatever— not God!).

"When we surrender, it is like signing a peace treaty: 'I am willing to stop fighting and allow people/places/things to be exactly as they are.' "

Notice that this woman accurately identifies the process of *allowing* life to happen. She has given up her futile attempts to try to control and change people and situations. Having embraced her femininity, she is better able to accept life as she finds it. This yielding quality brings a sense of peace and harmony to one's personal life, for its underlying dynamic is that of love. Only a loving woman can yield in the name of love; a woman seized by her power drives will not. The latter type of woman often gets to be right; the former gets to be cherished.

THE POWER OF LOVE

It can be seen that embracing the feminine principle of "strength in yielding" allows an entirely different approach to life and imbues it with a different sort of meaning. There is no logic to the feminine approach; indeed, this approach often betrays all laws of logic and reason. The woman who chooses to operate out of her feminine center will find a power in love unlike any she has experienced before, and her capacity to draw on that power will increase as she learns over time to trust its innate wisdom.

But the wisdom of the body and of the feminine soul often feel quite alien to the contemporary Amazon Woman, whose needs for dominance and ruthless will to power cut her off from her potential for love and joy. Much of her psychic energy is invested in trying to *control* life rather than being *receptive* to it. Often her life consists of a frenzied round of goal-oriented activities, leaving little room for actual loving. According to Marion Woodman, "To receive is to allow life to happen, to open oneself up to love and the light, grief and loss."[5] Yet to be receptive to the male, to be receptive to *all* of him, the good and the bad, can severely test the Madonna aspect of womanhood. Resistance to this process of surrender will be strong in many women, and this resistance must be experienced, analyzed, and integrated into the whole of the personality. One of my callers on the radio put it this way:

"I can't get away from resenting all the compromises I have to make. It feels as if women still have to do all the work to make a relationship happen. I thought we had come so far, and here we are back at square one, at least with men. I guess we do have more options than before. I mean, we can get out if we want to. But get out and go where? To our lonely rooms with our cats? I guess there just are no perfect men—they all require a tremendous amount of patience and faith and dedication and hope. And one reason I'm so angry about this is that I am so tired already. Maybe if I weren't so stressed out from my job I would have more energy to invest in what is apparently another type of career."

This woman does not yet have a loving attitude toward relationship. There is some truth to her statements, yet it is also clear that she has much to learn about the process of loving surrender, which still feels like work to her. And the reason it feels like work to her is because of her *resistance* to it; where there is defensive resistance to yielding, the process will indeed seem arduous. Surrender with the right man (and it is assumed here that one has chosen one's hero well) should feel like a joy and a triumph, for the dividends which accrue to the woman come not only from the increased love and tenderness which she receives from her man, but from her renewed sense of life itself.

DEEP BREATHING

First, however, the woman must be willing to let go, to simply allow life to happen in a relaxed and open way. On a physical level, something as simple as deep breathing can be enormously helpful in the surrender process. Marion Woodman, in *Addiction to Perfection*, observes that many of her overstriven analysands have been literally holding their breath for most of their lives. For these highly defensive women, "to let go, to simply let things happen, would be to surrender to the enemy."[6] A relaxed mental and physical attitude will enable a woman more readily to accept the flaws in the man with whom she wants union and surrender. But this openness and receptivity can appear frightening at first and may seem difficult to achieve.

Characteristically, the contemporary woman may feel frustrated with her slow progress, for, in typical Amazon fashion, she will wish to be experiencing everything all at once. But the shift in consciousness from power to love, from the masculine principle to the feminine, is a slow and gradual one, often filled with conflict and ambivalence.

Initially, there is often a sense of nothingness or defeat. Recall again Hippolyta's comment upon her initial surrender to Theseus, "I am nothing." The fear is always that if one is simply being and not doing, one will disintegrate, one will become a non-entity. Often there is a sense of wounded pride and anger. All of this must be dealt with, and each woman must feel these feelings and deal with these conflicts in her own individual way. In my experience, illness is not uncommon, especially respiratory illnesses (blocking of the breathing passages), and should be understood as a resistance to the surrender process.

It is important to note that the feminine instincts must not only be felt and experienced; they must also be *incorporated* with the masculine into the whole of one's personality. To merely live out formerly unconscious aspects of personality is not to integrate them fully into the self. Integration of femininity requires bringing *true consciousness* (here's where the Amazon is genuinely helpful) to the primitive, yet greatly feared feminine instincts, allowing the ego to reorganize them in a way that is comfortable to the individual. In short, this means that one does not take one's newly found feminine capabilities for surrender and express them crazily or impulsively. In Woodman's words, it means to "put the rider on the horse and let the rider make the decisions."[7]

Mistakes will be made. In all behavior change there is a tendency toward excessiveness; all revolutionaries have a touch of the zealot in them. Soon, however, the pendulum will swing back to a more comfortable place, and a sense of harmony between mind and body will start to occur. The woman then becomes capable of a relationship with a man and the world based on empathy, compassion, and understanding rather than on dependence or power. She is then truly acting out of her own center, her own sense of individuality as a woman and as an integrated person.

"KISS ME KATE!"

The Taming of the Shrew by William Shakespeare is a classic story of a difficult surrender. While Katherine, the heroine of the play, does not carry a briefcase (nor its sixteenth-century equivalent), she is an Amazon Woman in attitude: castrating, shrewish, sharp-tongued, highly dominant, opinionated, self-centered, and unwilling to let any man tell her what to do.

Kate's father, frustrated with her and needing to marry her off in order that his younger daughter might wed, offers an extremely large dowry to any man in the town willing to "tame" her and take her for his wife. Enter Petruchio, a bold and lusty man-about-town just a little bit down on his luck financially. He promises her father to "tame the shrew" in the name of perfect love, vowing that Kate will soon willingly surrender to him as her "lord and husband."

The middle of the play is characterized by a series of hilarious knock-down-drag-out fights, verbal assaults, insults, punishment, deprivation, humiliation, and all manner of manipulation. It is important to note, however, that Petruchio tames the difficult Kate through kindness and example, not through violence. In a myriad of ways, he shows her the inconvenience of her will to power; Kate soon sees that a soft voice and an amiable manner are far preferable to a sharp tongue and a violent temper. Petruchio is not always subtle; sometimes his "lessons" to her are maddeningly blatant, as when he insists that the moon is shining when it is, in fact, the sun.

PETRUCHIO: Come on, o' God's name: once more toward our father's.
Good Lord, how bright and goodly shines the moon!

KATHERINE: The moon! The sun: it is not moonlight now.

PETRUCHIO: I say, it is the moon that shines so bright.

KATHERINE: I know, it is the sun that shines so bright.

PETRUCHIO: Now, by my mother's son, and that's myself,
It shall be moon, or star, or what I list,[8]

This ridiculous exchange goes on for three more lines, after which time Hortensio entreats Katherine to concede to Petruchio lest they never get their journey under way. Finally, in frustration, Katherine concedes.

KATHERINE: Forward, I pray, since we have come so far,
And be it moon, or sun, or what you please.
And if you please to call it a rush-candle,
Henceforth, I vow, it shall be so for me.[9]

But even this is not enough. Having gotten Kate to agree that the moon was shining when indeed it was the sun, Petruchio does a quick about-face, looks up at the sky and calls her a liar, claiming that any fool could see that it is the "blessed sun" that is shining. Kate, however, has now learned the name of this game, and responds appropriately:

KATHERINE: Then God be blessed, it is the blessed sun:
But sun it is not, when you say it is not,
And the moon changes even as your mind.
What you will have it named, even that it is;
And so it shall be for Katherine.[10]

How did it happen that this witty, bright, and seemingly indomitable woman comes to a point where she recognizes the value *to her* in surrender to Petruchio? The play is not explicit on this point, although, clearly, Kate has found a kind of tranquility and peace which she was unable to experience while in combat with her man. While she has not lost her fiery spirit, she has discovered that it is easier to love and be loved by Petruchio than to fight with him.

Interestingly enough, the townspeople actually admire the fact that Kate has gone full cycle, from shrew to loving wife. They find her far more worthy of admiration than women who have always been docile. Kate has come to understand the power of femininity in a way that a naturally feminine woman could not because she can contrast it with the more masculine attitudes and behaviors she so recently and reluctantly relinquished. Kate now chooses to use her formidable intelligence and energy in support of her husband rather than in combat against him.

The climax of the play occurs in Kate's rousing speech to the women of the town, imploring them to embrace their femininity and surrender lovingly to their men:

"Thy husband is thy lord, thy life, thy keeper,
Thy head, thy sovereign; one that cares for thee,
And for thy maintenance; commits his body
To painful labour, both by sea and land,
To watch the night in storms, the day in cold,
Whilst thou liest warm at home, secure and safe;
And craves no other tribute at thy hands,
But love, fair looks, and true obedience,
Too little payment for so great a debt."[11]

But wait. That was *then*. Women today do not "liest warm at home, secure and safe"; most of them are out there hustling just like the men. Unfortunately for contemporary women, times have changed, but men and women haven't. The shrewish wife, employed in the world or at home, is still a living death to all around her, for no harmony exists while her will to power prevails. Kate says she is "ashamed, that women are so simple to offer war, where they should kneel for peace."[12]

Strange and exciting things, what the Jungians call "synchronicity," start to happen when a woman starts to open herself to peace and love, integrating the feminine aspects into her personality. The men in her life start to change, too. More actualized and mature men start to enter her life, men who are also struggling for consciousness in their relationships. Much like Petruchio, these men can greatly facilitate the process of the woman in transition. The internal psychological transformation which accompanies surrender can be greatly aided by a "willing and enthusiastic Petruchio who has the guts to put a bullet right through the heart of her King Kong animus. Whether he does that with anger or with unrelenting courage and faith depends on his nature, her nature and the nature of their relationship."[13]

However the man does this or, more accurately, the woman allows him to do this, there is no question but that the woman is involved in a type of voluntary submission. This is a normal though poorly understood element in the feminine psyche which has been referred to in psychoanalytic terms as "female masochism."

"I WANT WHAT YOU WANT"

What, really, is "masochism"? Most people associate masochism with pleasure and pain, images being conjured up of the abused and the abuser. In reality, however, this notion is far off the mark. Masochism can be more correctly viewed as the desire to endure pain rather than inflict it; to relinquish control rather than seize it; to surrender to life rather than manipulate it. In this sense, certainly, most women are indeed masochistic. For it is in the nature of woman to create and preserve life at all costs. On a monthly basis, she must yield to the reality of her menstrual cycle; in childbirth and in pregnancy, she must again yield herself up to forces beyond her control. All of this is accompanied by pain, a type of pain known only to women. And every well-integrated woman knows that to resist the pain is to increase it. One must learn to "go with the flow," surrender to it, ride the crest of the wave and come out the other end victorious. Women know that "love is long-suffering" and women surrender in love in a way which men can never understand.

Yet women also triumph in love, for through their willingness to surrender, they tie the bonds of relatedness extremely tight. This is why the truly feminine woman often will say, "I want what you want" to her man. If he likes her in red, red is what she will wear. If he dislikes flying, she will soon find herself taking trains. If he takes his toast with butter on it, margarine will disappear from her table. The more she surrenders to him, whether she intends to or not, the more she wants what he wants.

This process of surrender is so powerful, it seems almost magical. It is what makes a man feel that a woman is uniquely his, endears her to him, and makes him want to take care of her. In this way, a close bond of intimacy and trust—a sense of unity, of oneness—is established between the two lovers. Often when a woman tells a man that she wants what he wants, he will then decide—perhaps unconsciously—that he wants what she wants, that he wants nothing more than to provide her with everything she wants.

Or he could become a "pig," abusive and demanding. It is here where the woman must call upon her Black Madonna and set limits to which she holds firm. Women with an integrated sense of self and strong moral precepts have no problem in knowing what these limits are. Other women could have great difficulty in this regard and may require psychotherapy in order to learn where to draw the line with men who demand too much of them. Physical abuse is a red flag which should never be ignored; a woman should stop the process of surrender instantly at this point and terminate the relationship. Pathological behaviors must be distinguished from normal attempts on the part of the male to control his environment; in extreme cases, this may require the aid of a professional.

Most women, however, have an intuitive sense of when this line is crossed. With normal expressions of male dominance, a woman may experience a variety of feelings, ranging from thinly veiled amusement and tolerance to mild irritation to inflamed outrage. But in the presence of a disturbed and dangerous male, the key feeling that the woman consistently experiences is one of *fear*. Basically, a bad man gets his way through fear and intimidation. A Good Man, like Petruchio, does not have to frighten a woman in order to control her; he knows how to negotiate for power with love.

When a woman loves a man and truly wants to bond with him, she must take back her unreal projections of who she *wants* him to be and accept him as he really is. This is surrender; this is not imbuing a man with Ghostly Lover characteristics, not asking him to live up to hidden expectations, but accepting him as she finds him and rejoicing in all that he is.

"BETTER OFF WITHOUT HIM"

Divesting herself of unrealistic expectations is very difficult the contemporary Amazon Woman, for her Ghostly Lover is so riveting. He will not allow her to surrender to "another man." As we saw in Chapter Seven, instead of accepting, admiring, and appreciating her man, the modern woman often becomes highly critical, denigrating, and ultimately castrating. A man will characteristically retreat after such an assault, only to have the woman loudly declare to her Amazon friends that she is "better off without him."

These contemporary Moon Maidens of Artemis are often quick to agree; they secretly fear losing their dependable and available companion and friend to an "insensitive" male competitor. Years ago, the opposite was true; women understood and supported each other in the process of surrender to worthy men, for bonding with men was seen as *central* to a fulfilling and successful life.

Amazon mothers can also be instrumental in sabotaging the modern woman's attempts at surrender to a man. Take the case of C., a twenty-nine-year-old Amazon Woman abstract artist, who, before "melting her Amazon armor," had never received gifts or any real type of protection or caretaking from a man. Like most artists, she struggled financially, but she was professionally well regarded and moderately successful. Independent of spirit and sexually aggressive, she chose her lovers at her whim, only to find herself at age twenty-nine still alone in a studio apartment straining to make ends meet, and starting to panic about her future.

C. began to reflect upon her value system and her deepest needs in order to find a man with whom to spend the rest of her life. In doing so, she realized she needed to develop her repressed femininity. She soon found she experienced herself in a new way and related to men in a gentler, more receptive manner. Many fine men whom she would have formerly rejected now became attractive to her, and soon she had two eligible men in her life, both of whom seemed interested in marriage. For the first time, having embraced her femininity, she seemed to inspire some level of caretaking from men. When N. (with whom she had not even yet gone to bed) offered her his credit card and said, "Buy something to wear for our dinner Sunday night," she felt like a young girl on her first date. In a burst of exhilaration, she ran to the phone to tell her mother, only to hear her reply, "What? Give it back immediately! Who does he think he is? Doesn't he think you can *take care of yourself*?"

What this Amazon mother meant was: "How dare he think he's a better man than you are!" In reality, this young woman was struggling financially and welcomed her new suitor's generous gesture. She was *not* a better man than he, and this was part of her excitement about him, not just financially but on other levels as well. He was dynamic, aggressive, in charge of his world. He was willing and able to bring her into *his* territory, not move into hers. In short, he was an Actual Man, the first she had magnetized into her life since she was a teenager. But her mother, who, like most women of her generation, had lived a lifetime with an Actual Man, did not see male protection and support as important to the well-being of her daughter. She wanted for her daughter that which she had lacked in her own life: independence.

The "independence" of the Amazon Woman is, of course, an illusion. She may be independent from men, but she is extremely dependent upon her Ghostly

Lover, her friends, her work—as well as on her mother. Psychologists call the relationships of mature adults "interdependent," that of two independent persons who can allow themselves to depend on one another. In other words, they are capable of taking care of themselves but choose instead to help take care of each other. As people mature in life, they move, we hope, from a position of dependence (in infancy and childhood) to independence (in adolescence and early adulthood) to interdependence (in mature adulthood). And this experience of interdependence is best expressed and realized in an intimate and committed love relationship.

One of the hallmarks of healthy human development is the capacity to bond. And bond we must, consciously or unconsciously. Emotional self-sufficiency is an illusion; if we do not bond to men, we will bond to women, to our work, or to our fantasies.

TERMS OF SURRENDER

But no surrender is unconditional—in war or in love. All surrender has its terms, and each woman must decide for herself what her terms are. Surrender she must, but, as indicated in Chapter Six, the woman does have the opportunity to *choose the man*. When one considers that the man of one's choice must be viewed as a hero to whom one will surrender much personal control over the years, the choice of a hero becomes vitally important. This, then, is the first crucial step, the thoughtful and appropriate choice of a hero, a man whose manhood the woman is willing to support. If the woman is to view marriage as "forever," this first step of true surrender can be awesome and must be undertaken with extreme care.

Once the choice of hero has been made, terms of surrender must be negotiated. The woman who gives her body to a man before she even begins to negotiate the terms, as most contemporary women do, is taking a risk. She surrenders her body (and sometimes even her soul), then months, or even years, later, she may want to *renegotiate* the terms of surrender, not realizing that the deal has been closed.

Before giving a man everything, body *and* soul (which is what surrender is all about), a woman should have in her mind a sense of what it is she really wants and expects of the man. Many women remain vague on this point, claiming that all they really want is a compatible relationship, while in reality, they secretly long for marriage. But gone are the "good old days," when surrender, physical and emotional, followed marriage (although some women are going back to this). Most contemporary men have grown accustomed to the availability and easy sexuality of the modern woman and may not offer marriage or commitment prior to sexual involvement. Given these changes in social and sexual mores, many women of today feel that they both need and want to surrender physically to men prior to marriage. This does somewhat limit a woman's negotiating capacity, but physical surrender need not be spiritual. A woman can give her body, but should retain her *soul* until the man's devotion is as strong as hers.

Listen to the "success story" of T., an attractive but never-married thirty-seven-year-old cardiologist:

"I had been dating a man quite steadily for ten months. He was really the man of my dreams. I loved him madly, but could never tell him so. I never stopped competing with him; I guess I just couldn't surrender emotionally. I kept my feelings to myself, waiting for him to express his. Every time he told me about one of his other girlfriends, I told him about one of my boyfriends. Whenever he boasted about his material acquisitions, I topped him with tales of my own.

"Our relationship was sexually exciting and intellectually stimulating but never could seem to get off the ground emotionally. Everything came to a head when he announced his engagement to another woman—a real bimbo! My first impulse was to say I was marrying someone else *too*! But I couldn't. Instead, I burst into tears. I told him, 'I love you! You've meant so very much to me, more than I could ever say.' Through my tears, I told him how much a part of me he was. To my astonishment, he quietly responded, 'I love you, too.' This 'melted my Amazon armor'; I was so filled with tenderness for him, I just wanted to be 'his woman.' I started to yield on small points, trivial matters, sort of just laughed them off or serenely rose above them. In retrospect, I can see that my surrender began by 'opening up' and expressing my feelings for him. My reward was his returning these feelings. Having taken a chance and discovered that he loved me too, I was encouraged to continue my surrender to him, choosing love over power.

"One month later, he broke his engagement. In the interim, my expression of feelings and my new behaviors brought us much closer together. He told me that he was seeing a 'softer side' of me now, a side that he liked very much. He started to care for and take care of me in a way he never had before, calling me frequently, buying me gifts, giving me advice. For the first time in my adult life, I felt more like a woman with him, not just a doctor or a 'peer.' "

But the story does not end here. This newly awakened woman, transformed by the power of love and her own femininity, went on to utilize this power to set limits on the relationship and negotiate for marriage. How she did this is discussed in Chapter Nine, for the woman who secretly longs for marriage, yet fails to negotiate for it, is indeed masochistic in the pathological sense of the word. The truly healthy feminine woman surrenders herself completely to love only if she is loved and cared for in return. The soul aspect of a woman is expressed behaviorally in her devotion to her man; indeed, when a woman truly gives herself to a man, she is viewed as his "soulmate." But to give a man all this without having a marital commitment from him is to surrender unconditionally, having won no victory for oneself. This is foolish, for in love, surrender for a woman should be a victory, not a defeat.

Let us move on, then, to our final chapter, which addresses the issue of fulfillment of femininity through marriage.

CHAPTER NINE

Amazon Lady:
Fulfilling Your Femininity
Through Marriage

"Wilt thou have this Woman to thy wedded wife, to live together after God's Ordinance, in the holy estate of matrimony? Wilt thou love her, comfort her, honor and keep her, in sickness and in health; and, forsaking all others, keep thee only unto her, so long as ye both shall live?

"The man shall answer, 'I will.' "

These are the words almost every woman longs to hear from her hero, but how to get him to say them? Women today continue to retain the romantic notion that men shall pursue them ardently, propose on bended knee, and sweep them off into the sunset. This, alas, is seldom the case, and many a woman finds herself spending time in a so-called "committed" relationship, still unable to entice her reluctant lover to the altar.

THE REWARDS OF MARRIAGE

Unquestionably, there are many types of relationship in which a man and a woman can share love, but none comes close to the challenge and satisfaction of marriage. Marriage, more than any other type of relationship, tests our capacity for utilizing and fulfilling all four aspects of feminine personality, especially the Madonna, the soul of woman. Most marriages are lovely at the start, filled with hope and promise. People marry for many reasons, love being only one among them. Companionship, intimacy, mutual respect, passion—all these and much more are part of the rich tapestry that creates the fabric of a good marriage. It is not within the scope of this book to explore the institution of marriage as a whole. Rather, consistent with our earlier chapters, it is my intention to examine woman's unique contribution to a successful marriage and the benefits, emotional and spiritual, which will accrue to her from this loving investment of self.

Not every love affair can or should turn into a marriage. The rewards of marriage have nothing to do, really, with the thrill of romantic love, which often fades. It is critical, of course, that there be some "chemistry," an attraction to the man, or the woman will find it difficult to effect a harmonious relationship with him. But the rewards of marriage have far more to do with daily companionship, mutual support, empathy, compassion, and quite simply, having a "best friend."

The single life does have its pleasures, as most "liberated" women of today can attest, but secretly most of us suspect, deep in our hearts, that, in the words of poet Judith Viorst, "Married Is Better."

Married is indeed what most women want to be; in spite of woman's recent fascination with the world of the impersonal, her heart still seems to long for bonding. If the excessive devotion of the fifties homemaker proved confining for many of our mothers, it can safely be said that the emotional and personal detachment of the eighties woman has proven equally restrictive for many of their daughters. While not every woman needs to be married, many a modern woman has found that loving the "man within" is less than satisfying. Success in career without success in the personal realm can feel like a shallow victory.

The famous quote from Byron, "Man's love is of man's life a thing apart,/'Tis woman's whole existence" would probably be met with laughter by many a contemporary Amazon Woman. Yet, every night on my radio program, I am struck by the consistent female preoccupation with love. Women today intuitively sense that they are "animus-possessed," locked in the steely grip of their masculine aspect. They long to be free of it, to be put back in touch with their feminine centers. Love is a burning issue for contemporary women, yet ironically, they often do not know *how* to love, for much of love is blind, irrational, contradictory to the logical and masculine approach to life they have adopted.

Today's woman wants to experience love but often doesn't know how to give it, how to be a truly loving woman. Although Eros—the principle of love—is at the heart of the feminine psyche, today's woman is often tragically blocked from this spiritual source. A woman's intuition used to be her greatest strength; now it's her weakest. How can we get back in touch with what used to come so naturally to women? How can we learn that which technically cannot be taught, that which is essentially an art, a feminine mystery?

In order to awaken and raise feminine consciousness, we first must dare to make the unteachable

teachable. One way to attempt this is to approach the fascinating art of Womanhood not so much as an art, but as a game, a woman's game. A game can be taught; an art is intuitive. A game involves consciousness, whereas an art is unconscious. Today's woman is so out of touch with her feminine feelings that the ancient art of femininity must be translated into a game in order to make her conscious of how to play it. The art may be mysterious, but the game can be explained.

Leading a man gently down the road toward commitment and matrimony requires the utmost in patience, timing, awareness, and sensitivity. As such, this delicate and challenging life task will require that the woman utilize all of her capabilities and bring into play all four aspects of her personality: Amazon, Mother, Madonna, and Courtesan. Marriage, as we have seen, doesn't often simply "happen" to a woman, but it does to a man. Usually, a man doesn't even know *how* it happens, because it is the *woman* who is orchestrating the relationship, unbeknownst to him. This is the so-called "iron hand in the velvet glove," and it is an accurate description of the powerful feminine woman, a woman who personifies the tenor of our times. I have chosen to call this bold yet feminine woman as "Amazon *Lady*," bringing into play a word which has long been out of favor. If modern woman has been "No Longer a Lady"— as indicated in Chapter Four—it is time she once again became one—an Amazon Lady—a modern-day woman who has lovingly and joyfully integrated all four aspects of womanhood into the whole of her personality. And this new Amazon Lady cares very much about bonding, and views the experience of getting and staying married as one of life's great challenges.

THE AMAZON IN THE SERVICE OF FEMININITY

It may come as a surprise to learn, having talked so much throughout this book about the importance of the feminine, that it is the Amazon aspect of personality that is critically important to the process of getting married. For marriage, if nothing else, requires careful thought and discrimination. It is certainly time that contemporary American women, who have focused their energies on the outside world, now utilize their Amazon in the service of their femininity. Like the great Oueen Hippolyta, whose Amazon life was transformed by love, today's Amazon Lady is challenged to yield to her feminine instincts and integrate her strength with her softness. And what better way can a woman integrate her personality and fulfill her femininity than to lovingly bond with a man and acquire the benefits and pleasures of husband, home and children?

The previous chapters of this book are meant to improve and enhance *any* love relationship. Chapter Seven, in particular, offers some practical suggestions for heightening a man's interest and paving the way toward a commitment from the hero of one's choice. Even a monogamous relationship, however, accompanied by high levels of passion, may not be enough to ensure a proposal of marriage (though it certainly represents a good beginning). Let us explore, then, some of the ways in which women might approach the delicate task of "getting married."

NEGOTIATING FOR MARRIAGE

Many contemporary women have, by choice, remained single through their twenties and thirties, thinking that marriage would happen for them, perhaps sometime in the future, when they were "ready." Contemporary women were led to believe that getting married was easy, and that careers were difficult. Much to their chagrin, many of these women discovered that careers, by contrast, were much easier to orchestrate and negotiate than a marital contract with a desirable man. While the concept of "negotiating for marriage" may strike one as unromantic, getting married, in reality, rarely happens by accident. Getting married begins not just by wanting to, but also by embracing the feminine mode which fosters and encourages loving connections with men. Getting married also requires a considerable amount of purpose and focus, perhaps even more than a woman may have formerly invested in her career. Most important, getting and staying married requires a transformation from an Amazon Woman to an Amazon Lady. This transformation involves the utilization and investment of all four aspects of womanhood: the Mother, Madonna, and Courtesan to create a loving connection, and the Amazon to achieve and sustain the final goal of marriage.

Some women don't have to negotiate for marriage, but most do. The average man is apt to view marriage as a trap ("the tender trap"), a curtailment of his precious freedom and closely guarded autonomy. He innately senses that a great deal of responsibility will come with marriage, along with, in most cases, children. These and many other reasons combine to make the male elusive, not to love, but certainly to marriage. Even a man in love will often resist marriage, perhaps never even bringing the subject up, while the woman, in classic Madonna fashion, patiently waits— and waits—for him to "pop the question."

THE MARRIAGEABLE MAN

If marriage is indeed a woman's goal, there are three major issues that her Amazon aspect must continually test and evaluate as a relationship develops over time. First, the woman must determine if the man she has chosen is *committable* (will he establish an exclusive, sexually monogamous relationship?). Second, she must determine if the man with whom she has established a commitment is *marriageable* (is he ready to get married?). Third, she must determine if her man, though committable and marriageable, is eager and willing to marry *her*.

A man who is genuinely interested in a women is usually willing to establish a monogamous relationship within three months of fairly steady dating. Much more time than this generally indicates a losing battle, a lack of genuine interest in the woman as a permanent partner. During this trial period, a woman must call heavily upon her Madonna virtues, never issuing ultimatums, making demands, or begging for more time and attention in any way. She is cheerful to be around, no matter how frequently or infrequently the man sees her. Most importantly, she discreetly sees other people too, for the secret of her waiting patiently is that, in fact, she does *not* wait, but persistently (though somewhat reluctantly) continues to invest herself elsewhere both personally and socially.

As indicated in Chapter Seven, many women resist this, claiming that no one else "turns them on" or makes them as happy as their special man. For even an Amazon Lady, when deeply in love, will have a tendency to drift into monogamy, although her man may not yet have asked this of her. This is a mistake, for the woman who is desired by other men is far more attractive than one who waits home by the phone.

"Create an auction!" an elegant gentleman friend of mine rather crassly replied when I inquired as to how a woman might best go about the business of getting married. He was one of the few men I interviewed who was willing to confess that a bit of healthy competition was the one thing that might throw him over the edge and lead him to a permanent commitment. Actual Men are competitive and controlling by nature. They do not like to lose that which they have come to treasure.

"Keeping options open" are three magic words which will help a woman cope with the early stages of a marital negotiation with a man in whom she is truly interested. This keeps the pressure off the man she would like as her husband and allows him the very important sense of pursuing *her*. The old saying "he chases her until she catches him" has real psychological validity in that it captures, in just a few words, the essence of the male-female dilemma. A man, in order to desire a woman as a marriage partner, must feel loved and appreciated by her. But he must also feel that he is the pursuer, she the not altogether willing object of his pursuit.

Having other relationships, interests, and friends helps to reduce anxiety and divert an Amazon Lady's natural tendency to close a negotiation for marriage too soon. Remember, a man must be given the illusion of control, not just in this matter, but in most matters throughout life. This is what Irene Claremont de Castillejo's mother must have meant when she counseled her, "One cannot knock one's husband down, but one has got to get round him somehow."[1] Other women have said it in other ways. The bottom line is this: A man will resist direct confrontation from a woman in almost any matter, but especially in a situation that will affect him for the rest of his life.

THE BIVALENT WOMAN

A woman, then, in order to be most attractive to a man as a marriage partner, is best advised to adopt, if at all possible, what I call a bivalent attitude, an attitude thought to be typical of the truly feminine woman: She will, she won't, she might, and she might not. This attitude is experienced as challenging to most men, for it allows a man the feeling of chasing, directing, and ultimately capturing the woman.

Is this manipulation? Perhaps. But it is manipulation of the most benign nature, manipulation in the name of love. Furthermore, it is a type of manipulation that men enjoy and expect of women. Secretly they are flattered by it, and, if truly in love, capitulate to it.

The woman who desires marriage, but does not yet have a commitment, should go out with other men— perhaps platonically—but make it clear to her special man that her preference is to be with him and him alone. If the man is falling in love, he will resent the competition and try to eliminate it. Some men will attempt to do so unilaterally, i.e., they will try to convince the woman to stop seeing other men but will not agree to stop seeing other women in return. If this occurs, the woman's Madonna must stand firm. Commitment and monogamy must be bilateral and mutually agreed to by both parties.

Women who have difficulty with this step may have to face the fact that they are choosing their heroes poorly or unrealistically. Such a woman might reread Chapter Six and ascertain whether she might still be in search of a Ghostly Lover, a man she can never have. Perhaps she is still playing Blemish, criticizing the eligible men who are attracted to her. She must use her Amazon to take inventory of herself and determine whether she is being grandiose about who she is and what she deserves. Somewhere out there is a real man—a Good Man—who is ready and willing to make a commitment to her.

CREATING A COMFORT ZONE

Having patiently waited through the attachment period and succeeded in securing a commitment, many a contemporary woman still finds herself with a man who resists marriage. While living together should be avoided, a woman can use this tentative period in the relationship to her advantage if she provides her man with a pleasant taste of how comfortable daily life with her might be. One woman, who obviously succeeded in this regard, was told by her marriage-phobic lover, "You make me want to hang lace curtains." It would be helpful at this point to review

Chapters Five and Seven and recall the importance of each of the four aspects of female personality, especially the Madonna and the Courtesan, and the ways in which they are viewed through the eyes of men. Creating a "comfort zone," an environment of harmony and joy, is one of the most delicate and inspirational challenges of being a woman. Ideally, a discriminating and creative Amazon Lady can orchestrate the feminine aspects of her personality—the Mother, Madonna, and Courtesan—to create a harmonious and loving environment where, in spite of adversity, the music never stops playing.

TOP PRIORITY

Does all of this sound like a lot of work? Not at all, not compared to what many women put into other goals they want to achieve. A worthy man is indeed a worthy goal and should willingly be made a top priority in an Amazon Lady's life. Like the Amazon Queen Hippolyta, today's woman needs to learn that investment of self in a marriage (and a home and children) requires as dedicated an investment as that which she makes in her career. Each woman must decide for herself how she is to prioritize her time and energies. Personally, I have always admired the philosophy of Mary Kay, head of the Mary Kay Cosmetics empire: "God first, family second, job third." The modern Amazon Lady who operates first out of a spiritual center and stays in touch with her loving values is apt to be a far happier person with a greater probability of success, both professionally and personally.

Of course, not all investments of energy pay off, not in the world of the personal or the professional. The relationship which continues for more than a year after a commitment has been made may well be going nowhere. Hopefully, the man will approach the subject of marriage during this time period, but if he doesn't, the woman must. This may strike many women as overly dynamic and aggressive; it is not. The man, it must be remembered, has already been magnetized. The woman who then fails to negotiate for what she wants (marriage) is not dealing from a position of strength and may be suffering from profound insecurity and low self-steem.

"We have been together for close to a year now," she might begin. "I love you madly (passionately, completely). But I feel the need to be married." It is important not to issue either/or ultimatums, threats, or demands. Remembering man's castration anxiety and pride, a woman must somehow communicate that she is courageously attempting to take care of *her* needs, not trying to intimidate the man into doing something he does not want to do.

This is a risk, since there is a chance that the man might refuse. Still, it is a risk worth taking, for libidinal energy which is tied up in an unmarriageable man is libidinal energy (and time) wasted. It is at such a juncture in a woman's life that she can feel grateful if she has retained friendships with other men, who, at this point, may begin to look more attractive to her.

Love, it is true, takes time to grow. But a lengthy monogamous commitment without definite plans for marriage is little more than a prolonged sort of adolescent "going steady." This is fine when you're sweet sixteen, but not when you are a mature adult. It is not uncommon to find contemporary men and women "playing house," "hanging out," or "keeping comany," moving past the appropriate time in a relationship when marriage should have occurred.

SETTING A WEDDING DATE

Some men, when asked to set a wedding date, will attempt to negotiate for more time, and three months might be considered a reasonable period for further contemplation. Do, however, have *some* time limit fixed in your mind; again, the Madonna in the woman must be strong. Be prepared to walk away—permanently—if a marital commitment is not forthcoming. Try to part tenderly, without bitterness or anger. "I must get on with my life. I need to see other men and fall in love again." *Do so*. Many men in these situations (commitment without marriage) secretly believe the woman is bluffing and will soon be back. Be sure to call this bluff, and bravely utilize your Amazon to get out in the world again, meet other men, mingle with other people, and generally keep busy. If a man is deeply attached to you, there is a good probability that he will try to retain contact through phone calls, flowers, etc.; a woman in love will tend to yield to these seductions and allow an occasional night of passion to break her resolve to move on in life. *Resist this temptation*. Remember the power of partial reinforcement as defined in Chapter Seven; seeing a man occasionally will only bind you to him more closely. Do not accept a man back into your life without a commitment to marriage and a definite wedding date.

A man whose intentions with a woman are serious will generally propose or agree to marriage within one year of knowing her. If he doesn't, a woman is well advised to cut her losses and let him go. Such a man is simply not marriageable, at least not to this woman, or not at this time. In love, it has been said that timing is everything. The Jungians call this "synchronicity," a coming together of people and events at the proper psychological and spiritual time. Sometimes the people are right but the timing is wrong. Other times, the man simply is not marriageable, not to her, not to anyone. In any event, holding on with the mistaken belief that he'll "come around" or change his mind is a waste of time and energy. A woman must take a man at his word. She must *believe him* when he says he does not want marriage, and get on with her life.

MOVING ON AND STAYING HOPEFUL

Practice makes perfect, even in the world of love. Having invested herself completely in a relationship, a woman, though disappointed and hurt, can feel some satisfaction in having offered a man her very best. The Amazon Lady who has embraced her femininity, integrated the four aspects of her personality, and related them lovingly to a man is *more of a woman* than the woman who has never tried at all. In addition, a near miss is marvelous preparation for the next win; the woman disappointed in love should stay in a marrying mood and bring all her feminine charms to the next hero of her choice, who may find them— and her—irresistible.

Woman's unique role as mediator to man has not

changed markedly over the centuries and is not likely to change, for man will continue to look to woman as his "better half," as a conduit to his feelings, his thoughts, indeed, his very soul. Marriage must once again be recognized as a career for a woman, a type of work worthy of her time, attention, and energy. And if indeed marriage is "women's work," men would be well advised to choose a woman with care, for it is a sacred trust that they give unto her keeping. For if a woman does not "keep" a marriage, nobody will. Carol Gilligan and others have gathered impressive developmental data to suggest that this orientation toward relationship is inherent to our sex. Staying married requires the love and devotion of both a man and a woman, but it still seems to be the woman who pays closer attention to the personal needs and feelings of the people in her environment.

BEING A WOMAN—FOREVER

Embracing femininity means embracing it for life; whatever attitudes and behaviors a woman projects at the beginning of a relationship with her special man, her hero, should be maintained for the rest of their lives together. The same qualities that make marriages happen also make marriages last. For staying married is even more complex and challenging than getting married; this book cannot begin to address the many areas of marriage in which a man and a woman can grow and change together over the course of a lifetime. But, as always, it is the Madonna and Courtesan aspects of the woman which remain critically important to her successful relating to man, and it is because of deficiencies in these areas that marriages either don't happen, or ultimately falter and die. Only two of these failures shall be addressed here: (1) failure to maintain harmony in the home (the Madonna role) and (2) failure to keep the flame of love alive (the Courtesan role).

SINGING HARMONY

A great wife is analogous to a great harmony singer. What she does requires a kind of suspension of the ego, a relinquishing of personal power in the service of creating an even more vibrant and exciting sound. There is a subtle yet profound power in singing harmony. How cold and strident the lead singer sounds all by himself; how exquisite he sounds when the perfect harmonizer is chiming in on just the right notes.

In harmony singing, the object is to make the other person sound better. In harmony living, the object is to make the other person feel better. Harmonizing involves a willingness to surrender one's own ego to the needs of the other. It's what my mother always called having a "sense of otherness." Singing harmony—or living harmony—requires paying a lot of attention to the other. The lead singer may look out into the audience, but the harmony singer must look in, following the lead.

A woman can't do this with every man; that is, harmony can't be sung with just anybody. A woman can only sing harmony with a man whose lead she is willing and able to follow, a man she can continue to admire and regard as her hero over a lifetime, in spite of the fact that her strength may often be greater than his and her wisdom more profound. Her mission in her feminine role is to make him look and feel better, to enhance his masculinity and sense of self-worth, both in his eyes and in the eyes of the world. And in this feminine loving, there is peace and there is power. Keeping the music playing in marriage is one of the great challenges of being a woman and requires the utilization of all four aspects of female personality. Singing harmony means paying close attention to the lead singer and never forgetting who that lead singer is. It's time once again to seize the privileges and the power that go with letting the man lead, with being a man's woman, *your* man's woman.

THE FUTILITY OF FIGHTING

Chronic fighting is anathema to any relationship, yet many couples bicker and fight constantly. My father used to say, "A team of horses cannot withdraw the spoken word." The castrating, swordlike quality of the animus-possessed female tongue is legendary; a woman is well advised to save herself the pain of cutting words which she may desperately wish to withdraw and which he will never forget. This can be difficult, for we are human, not saints; when we remember to operate out of a position of love instead of power, however, this becomes easier and the rewards are plentiful. Grave psychological damage is done with the expression of anger, the results of which can be devastating and irreparable. Utilizing the Madonna, learning to repress one's anger, is a far greater victory, resulting more often than not in the restoration of love and harmony in the home.

Receptivity is one of the hallmarks of the feminine

consciousness; *being* over *doing,* allowing life to just happen. Nowhere, perhaps, is the modern woman more challenged to test her feminine powers than when in disagreement with her husband or lover. The best way to deal with an impending argument is simply to be there, and know that it will pass. Most arguments are about trivia, inconsequential matters that have no meaning in the grand scheme of things; nonetheless, these minor disputes can slowly erode and eventually destroy the fabric of a relationship.

OUTLASTING HIM WITH LOVE

Any fool can and will argue night and day with a man. It takes a smart and strong woman to outlast him, not with anger, but with love. Before the current Crisis in the Madonna, women were better at this than men, and men knew it. They were awed by a woman's patience, perseverance, serenity, and altruism in the face of stress and adversity. What they didn't realize—and what perhaps women then and certainly today may not have realized—was that ultimately this altruism was selfish. One great Mother-Madonna of yesteryear explained it to me this way:

"It took me years to learn to be patient, to bite my tongue, to overlook his many faults and idiosyncrasies. My husband is not an easy man to live with, but then what man is? Over time, I came to see that it was the only way, the only way I could be the victor. It was for *me,* really, not for him. It was for my marriage and for my children. It was to preserve the love between us, and I *have* preserved it for over thirty years now, and he knows very well that I'm very much the reason why."

A woman makes or breaks the harmony of the home. The power is in her hands. Men have indeed entered the world of the feminine, the world of relatedness and of feelings, but they have not done so with any real impact or strength. As pointed out earlier, when men embrace the feminine, they sometimes do so with a woman's softness but not with her strength; when women enter the masculine realm, they tend to do so with a man's hardness but not with his kindness. When men and women bicker and fight, they tend to do so out of the worst aspects of themselves; he out of his moody anima, she out of her bellicose animus.

Women who refuse to embrace the feminine role are often characterized by a rigid personality structure. Their need to be right is greater than their need to be loved; they resent the traditional feminine role of keeping the peace and singing harmony. It is the Amazon part of the woman which needs to be right, which is often brutally honest, the part of her which is direct, clear-sighted, forceful, confrontational, and aggressive. A well-balanced Amazon Lady has learned how to temper her Amazon with her Mother-Madonna aspect, which is merciful. This feminine compassion and tenderness are desperately needed by men, who are not likely to encounter it in their day-to-day existence. The woman who is "honest" may be "right," but in the realm of the personal she is seldom a comfort to anyone. "Being there" with an open heart and mind is much of the secret to being a woman and often can accomplish more in transforming the lives of others than any form of open confrontation.

Fighting with men should be avoided not just to

preserve male pride, but also to preserve female dignity. There is nothing less attractive or uninviting than the frenzied or crazed woman, the proverbial fishwife who uses the power of her tongue instead of the power of her femininity. Fighting makes a woman ugly to men, and ugly to herself. Much has been written in the popular psychological literature about the value of releasing aggression. Little has been written about the value of suppressing it and choosing peace and love instead. Anger is often not cleansing; it is emotionally debilitating and erodes the fabric of a loving relationship.

But we are human, and sometimes we will fight. If a woman finds that she cannot remain silent or withdraw, it is best to say something like "I am too angry to talk just now" or "I am too hurt and confused to discuss this intelligently now." If you must express your feelings, express them with an "I" statement, not a "you" statement, for "you" statements usually are aggressive and often end up with name calling and accusations ("You idiot!"). Avoid, also, the Critical Parent words of "always" and "never." These words are invariably preceded by the word "you" ("You always . . . You never . . ."). No good can come from sentences begun this way.

We have seen thus far that fighting can be avoided through the silence of the Madonna or the carefully worded expression of feelings by the Amazon. Another way is through the Courtesan, by staying playful and keeping one's sense of humor even in the face of conflict. Many potentially volatile situations between men and women can be diffused with a lighthearted remark or a bit of playful teasing. One's husband, of course, should be taken seriously; his needs, his wants, his moods, his interests should all be of paramount importance, for he is your best friend, your lover, your life companion, your protector. On the other hand, on a daily basis, the small and trivial issues of life must be dealt with lightly, for they are indeed not serious. The woman who takes things seriously can find herself constantly in a state of crisis. The woman who takes things lightly (utilizing the playfulness of the Courtesan and the patience of the Madonna) radiates happiness and creates an atmosphere of joy all around her.

KEEPING THE FLAME OF LOVE ALIVE

A woman most often represents the "glue" of an enduring relationship. Once again, we return to the concept of Eros as the quintessential feminine principle, i.e., love as the center of a woman's existence. But love is not just an issue central to women, or even an issue that occurs only between men and women; it is an issue central to life itself. Love is the essence of what is commonly known as "soul," both in men and in women. Yet love continues so often to be left to the woman's keeping; it seems still in the nature of things for man to look to woman as the keeper of his soul. And so it often still appears to be a woman's unique role to keep this flame alive, never to forget the importance of her role as woman in this regard.

And one thing is for certain: This flame of love will surely die if a woman becomes indifferent to her husband's sexual advances. Problems in sexuality begin when the man *stops* asking, and stop he will if a woman frequently refuses. Intercourse for a woman can indeed sometimes "move the earth"; at other times, it is little more than a kiss. What, really, is the difference over the course of a lifetime? Every sexual act can and should be different; all sexuality, however, should be viewed as part of loving.

Sex, for a woman, is relatively effortless, requiring less energy than walking up three flights of stairs or cooking a casserole. Why not be physically close when your man is in the mood? Many a modern woman, upon hearing this counsel, is horrified, loudly proclaiming that she does not wish to be viewed (in the words of a recent caller) as "just a receptacle." *I* was horrified at this image for what is supposed to be an act of love between a man and a woman, an act in which a woman need not always be erotically or sexually aroused, but one in which she can certainly be receptive and loving.

Waning or erratic virility and sexual desire are a part of almost all marriages and occur in the young as well as the old at unpredictable intervals. Generally, young men are more sexually active than old, though this may not always be the case. Often, mature women report that their husbands are even more interested in sexual experimentation as they find themselves with more time and leisure; such women may be challenged to explore and perhaps reawaken the Courtesan aspects of their personalities. Even more difficult is dealing with the husband who has withdrawn sexually or may be suffering from a sexual dysfunction. Here, the woman must decide whether to utilize her Madonna or her Courtesan aspect in dealing with the dilemma. The man who is fatigued, stressed, depressed, or distracted is best left alone sexually and treated with empathy, tenderness, and kindness. Men do suffer, more than they will admit, from variability in their sexual needs and drives; it is most important that a woman utilize her Madonna and show loyalty and compassion for her man during these times when he may be questioning his "manhood."

YOUR DATE FOR LIFE

Where sex in a marriage has simply grown old or stale, however, the woman would do well to examine herself and the nature of the relationship. Has there been undue bickering and nagging? Have you remembered to compliment and admire him? Does he still feel *appreciated* by you as a man, as your hero? If the answers to all of these questions are yes, you might then ask yourself if your Courtesan is still alive for both of you, if you are still the woman he once loved to make love to. A woman can be sexually enticing at any age, but she must work at it, giving it the same time and attention she would give an important aspect of her career. Remember that your husband is your date for life, and treat him as such.

It is helpful in a marriage to pause from time to time and reflect upon the reasons why you married your man in the first place. There is every possibility that these reasons still exist. Many times, when a woman complains bitterly on the radio to me about the difficulties of living with her husband, I inquire as to the reasons why she married him in the first place. Often it is astonishing to hear the marvelous and touching things which the woman then reveals to me. Usually, I then go on to inquire whether her husband still possesses these qualities; invariably the answer is "yes." But if time and the stresses of daily living have obscured the wonderful traits you once admired in your man, make it your goal to reawaken and rediscover them, for they are dormant within him and can be brought back to life with your love.

Pay attention as your man grows and changes over the years; the woman who is not sensitive to growth and change in her husband as the years pass is almost certain to lose or to alienate him. Understanding his moods, his fears about employment, his questioning of his manhood and of life, this and much more are a critical part of being a woman and keeping the fabric of marriage from wearing thin. Boredom and routine are the great enemies of marriage and result from the failure of men and women truly to pay attention to each other after a long period of time. This is commonly known as being taken for granted. Indeed, it is easy to take the other person for granted over time, assume he will always be there, and fail to develop oneself emotionally, intellectually, and sexually.

Why does a woman do these things? Because she loves her man, she wants to keep him, but most of all because it enhances her femininity, brings her joy, and increases her sense of power as a woman. It is pleasant, it is satisfying, it is nourishing to yield in the name of love. A woman cannot help but feel angry and inadequate when she is failing in her personal life. Triumph in love is a high adventure, unlike any other; women today are wanting to succeed in the world of the feminine, to enjoy the thrill of victory in love.

GROWING INTO WOMANHOOD

Growing into one's womanhood and embracing all four aspects of feminine personality—this has been a challenge for women of every generation, not just ours. Listen to the tale of P., a fifty-one-year-old woman who married at eighteen and quickly bore three children before she had developed much of an individuated personality.

"Really, I don't know how my husband stood me in the early days of our marriage. I was such a baby. If I didn't get my own way, I threw a temper tantrum, just like a child. I yelled and screamed, slammed doors, and sometimes walked out. I was impossible to talk to. Looking back, I'm extremely grateful for his patience with me; otherwise, our marriage could not have survived. Finally, after about eight years of this, I just got sick of myself. I went back to school to raise my self-esteem and find an outlet outside the home. Most of all, I just decided to stop fighting and restore harmony with my man. I needed to grow up, to stretch myself intellectually, and stop taking out my resentments and frustrations on my husband."

Clearly, a woman's personality can grow and develop in many ways. This woman went on to shed further light on how she and her husband adapted to each other as the years passed:

"Working outside the home presented new challenges for me. At the end of the day, my tendency was to come home and dump all my troubles on my husband. Finally, he started to say, 'See if you can save it until Sunday morning.' And I always could. In fact, by Sunday morning, all the problems were usually gone. One of the reasons why I succeeded in making all these transitions in my life was that I remained devoted to my husband and my marriage; I did not ignore him as I grew, but *paid attention* to the invaluable suggestions he made along the way, as well as his changing needs, and I did so without resentment. I really wanted to succeed in my marriage *and* in my work, and I feel that I have.''

So Long As Ye Both Shall Live . . .

Most men would be willing to support and encourage a woman in her work and her personal development if they felt continuing tenderness and devotion from her. But devotion does not mix well with the prevailing contemporary ethic of narcissism and self-fulfillment at all costs. Narcissism, self-love, is a trap, a black hole into which one can fall. Devotion, by contrast, is an escape *from* oneself; ideally, it can represent an opportunity to discover one's best self through love of another. Devotion especially involves the utilization of what I have called the Madonna aspect of the feminine personality, because it requires faith in the other person, the object of devotion. It requires faith through adversity. It requires faith through disappointment. It requires faith although all of one's needs are not being fulfilled. It requires faith in less than perfect situations. Most of all, it requires an altruistic giving of oneself to another. The beautiful words of the marriage ceremony, ''for richer or for poorer, in sickness or in health,'' imply a concept of enduring devotion and commitment which often runs counter to the liberated consciousness and ego demands of the contemporary woman. Yet devotion is essential to the soul of woman; without it, she can know little happiness.

For it is only in giving that we ultimately receive. Even Hippolyta, who found tremendous happiness as a woman with her own great King Theseus, had to give up much of the life she had known and enjoyed. She never did lose her Amazon ways completely. With her athletic prowess and disdain for female matters, she was considered a bit peculiar within the Athenian community. Nonetheless, she did embrace her femininity and devote herself to her King, bringing new energy and joy to palace life. She lovingly compromised her ways and moved into Theseus's world, bearing him a son and finding great peace and serenity with him. Toward the end of her life, when surrounded by the Amazon Moon Maidens, who shouted, "Hippolyta! Where is your faith?" she responded, "It is here! With my man and my King!"[2]

Through her love of a man, this great Amazon Oueen had developed and fulfilled her suppressed femininity; her journey through love had transformed her from an Amazon Woman to an Amazon *Lady*.

My notion of an Amazon Lady is consistent with the southern notion of the "Steel Magnolia": a woman of strength and sweetness. Barbara Walters is an excellent example of this kind of powerful yet feminine woman; so, too, are Elizabeth Taylor and Jacqueline Kennedy Onassis, each in a distinctive way. But one need not be a famous or high-profile person to aspire to this ideal of womanhood; indeed, every woman has the potential to become her own kind of Amazon Lady over the course of her lifetime.

The ideal woman of today is not the same as the ideal woman of yesteryear; she is *more*. And because she is more, her newfound Amazon strength must be balanced by an increase in her feminine energies. Without this balance, modern woman is deprived of her innate birthright, her feminine power. This is the challenge of every Amazon Woman today: To balance the strength of the steel with the sweetness of the magnolia, to become an Amazon Lady.

Fulfilling one's womanhood is a lifelong process, one which has been made more difficult by the masculine consciousness so many of us have adopted. Or perhaps it is really not more difficult at all, only more confusing, for we are more enlightened, more able to understand and feel the contradiction between the male and female elements within us. Modern woman may be better able to appreciate the victory she can feel in fulfilling her femininity, for she can contrast it with the emptiness she has experienced when she has not.

Being a woman today is a bold new adventure, with love and loving as its ultimate reward.

BIBLIOGRAPHY

Barbach, Lonnie. *For Yourself: The Fulfillment of Female Sexuality*. New York: Doubleday, 1975.

Berne, Eric. *Transactional Analysis in Psychotherapy*. New York: Grove Press, 1961.

————. *Games People Play: The Psychology of Human Relationships*. New York: Random House, 1964.

————. *Principles of Group Treatment*. New York: Grove Press, 1966.

————. *What Do You Say After You Say Hello? The Psychology of Human Destiny*. New York: Grove Press, 1972.

Blotnick, Srully. *Otherwise Engaged: The Private Lives of Successful Career Women*. New York: Facts on File Publications, 1985.

Brownmiller, Susan. *Femininity*. New York: Simon and Schuster, 1984.

Christ, Carol P. *Diving Deep and Surfacing: Women Writers on Spiritual Quest*. Boston: Beacon Books, 1980.

Cleckley, Hervey. *The Mask of Sanity*. New York: NAL, 1982.

Daniell, Rosemary. *Sleeping with Soldiers: In Search of the Macho Man*. New York: Holt, Rinehart and Winston, 1985.

221

De Beauvoir, Simone. *The Second Sex*. New York: Alfred A. Knopf, 1952.

De Castillejo, Irene Claremont. *Knowing Woman: A Feminine Psychology*. New York: Harper & Row, 1973.

Dimen, Muriel. *Surviving Sexual Contradictions: A Startling and Different Look at a Day in the Life of a Contemporary Professional Woman*. New York: Macmillan, 1986.

Friedan, Betty. *The Feminine Mystique*. New York: W. W. Norton, 1962.

————. *The Second Stage*. New York: Summit Books, 1981.

Gilligan, Carol. *In a Different Voice: Psychological Theory and Women's Development*. Cambridge, Mass.: Harvard University Press, 1982.

Glasser, William. *Reality Therapy: A New Approach to Psychiatry*. New York: Harper & Row, 1965.

Greer, Germaine. *The Female Eunuch*. New York: McGraw-Hill, 1970.

Harding, M. Esther. *The Way of All Women*. New York: Harper & Row, 1970.

Harlow, Harry, "The Nature of Love," *The American Psychologist*, 12:673–685, 1958.

————. "Social Deprivation in Monkeys," *Scientific American*, 207:136–46, November 1962.

Hewlett, Sylvia Ann. *A Lesser Life: The Myth of Women's Liberation in America*. New York: William Morrow, 1986.

Horner, Matina, "Femininity and Successful Achievement: A Basic Inconsistency," Chap. 3 in Bardwick, Douvan, Horner, and Gutmann, eds., *Feminine Personality and Conflict*. Belmont, Calif.: Brooks/Col, 1970.

————,"Why Bright Women Fear Success" in *The Female Experience*, from the Editors of *Psychology Today* (Del Mar, Calif.: CRM, 1973).

Jacobi, Jolande. *The Psychology of C. G. Jung*. London: Routledge and Kegan Paul, 1942.

James, Muriel, and Dorothy Jongward. *Born to Win: Transactional Analysis with Gestalt Experiments*. Reading, Mass.: Addison-Wesley, 1971.

Johnson, Robert A. *He: Understanding Masculine Psychology*. New York: Harper & Row, 1974.

————. *She: Understanding Feminine Psychology*. New York: Harper & Row, 1976.

————. *We: Understanding the Psychology of Romantic Love*. New York: Harper & Row, 1983.

Jung, Carl G. *The Archetypes and the Collective Unconscious*. Princeton, N.J.: Princeton University Press, 1959.

————. *Civilization in Transition: The Collected Works of C. G. Jung*, Vol. 10. Princeton, N.J.: Princeton University Press, 1964.

————. *Modern Man in Search of a Soul*. New York: Harcourt, Brace, and Company, 1933.

Kiley, Dan. *The Peter Pan Syndrome: Men Who Have Never Grown Up*. New York: Avon, 1983.

Klagsbrun, Francine. *Married People: Staying Together in the Age of Divorce*. New York: Bantam Books, 1985.

Lasch, Christopher. *The Culture of Narcissism: American Life in an Age of Diminishing Expectations*. New York: W. W. Norton, 1979.

Leonard, Linda. *The Wounded Woman: Healing the Father-Daughter Relationship*. Athens, Ohio: Swallow Press, 1982.

Lindbergh, Anne Morrow. *Gift from the Sea*. New York: Vintage Books, 1978.

Littwin, Susan. *The Postponed Generation. Why American Youth Are Growing Up Later*. New York: William Morrow, 1986.

McBroom, Patricia A. *The Third Sex: The New Professional Woman*. New York: William Morrow, 1986.

Miller, Alice. *Prisoners of Childhood: The Drama of the Gifted Child and the Search for the True Self*. New York: Basic Books, 1979.

Millett, Kate. *Sexual Politics*. New York: Doubleday, 1969.

Orsborn, Carol. *Enough Is Enough: Exploding the Myth of Having It All*. New York: G. P. Putnam's Sons, 1986.

Plath, Sylvia. *The Bell Jar*. New York: Harper & Row, 1971.

Renault, Mary. *The Bull from the Sea*. New York: Pantheon, 1962.

Sanford, John A. *The Invisible Partners: How the Male and Female in Each of Us Affects Our Relationships*. New York: Paulist Press, 1980.

Scarf, Maggie. *Intimate Partners: Patterns in Love and Marriage*. New York: Random House, 1987.

Scott-Maxwell, Florida. *Women and Sometimes Men*. New York: Alfred A. Knopf, 1937.

Shakespeare, William. *The Taming of the Shrew*. New York: Penguin, 1981.

Singer, June. *Androgyny: Toward a New Theory of Sexuality*. New York: Anchor Press/Doubleday, 1976.

Smith, Cynthia. *The Seven Levels of Marriage*. New York: Lyle Stuart, 1986.

Tzu, Sun. *The Art of War*. New York: Delacorte Press, 1983.

Viorst, Judith. *It's Hard to Be Hip over Thirty and Other Tragedies of Married Life*. New York: New American Library, 1970.

Von Franz, Marie-Louise. *Puer Aeternis: A Psychological Study of the Adult Struggle with the Paradise of Childhood*. Santa Monica, Calif.: Sigo Press, 1970.

Wolff, Toni, "Structural Forms of the Feminine Psyche," *Der Psychologe*, Heft 7/8, Bern, Switzerland, 1951.

Woodman, Marion. *Addiction to Perfection: The Still Unravished Bride*. Toronto: Inner City Books, 1982.

Woolf, Virginia. *A Room of One's Own*. New York: Harcourt Brace Jovanovich, 1957.

NOTES

Introduction

1. M. Esther Harding, *The Way of All Women* (New York: Harper & Row, 1970), p. xv. *Introduction* by C. J. Jung, Zurich, February 1932.

The Big Lies of Liberation: Modern Woman Led Astray

1. Simone de Beauvoir, *The Second Sex* (New York: Alfred A. Knopf, 1952).

2. Carol Gilligan, *In a Different Voice: Psychological Theory and Woman's Development* (Cambridge, Mass.: Harvard University Press, 1982), pp. 9–10.

3. Patricia A. McBroom, *The Third Sex* (*Wall Street Journal*, 1982); Neil G. Bennett, David E. Bloom, and Patricia A. Craig, *The Black and White Marriage Pattern: Why So Different* (New Haven, Conn.: Yale University Press, 1986).

Amazon Woman: Armed and Ready for Battle

1. Mary Renault, *The Bull from the Sea* (New York: Pantheon, 1962), p. 117.

2. Ibid., p. 119.

3. Ibid., pp. 133–134.

4. Ibid., p. 134.

5. Ibid., p. 138.

6. Ibid., p. 139.

7. Ibid., p. 150.

8. Ibid., p. 154.

9. Irene Claremont de Castillejo, *Knowing Woman* (New York: Harper & Row, 1973), p. 110.

10. I am indebted to Dr. Linda Leonard for her illuminating discussion of the "Armored Amazon." See *The Wounded Woman: Healing the Father-Daughter Relationship* (Athens, Ohio: Swallow Press, 1982), p. 61.

11. C. G. Jung, *Civilization in Transition,* Vol. 10 of *The Collected Works of C. G. Jung* (Princeton, N.J.: Princeton University Press, 1964), p. 260.

12. M. Esther Harding, *The Way of All Women* (New York: Harper & Row, 1970), p. 4.

THE FOUR ASPECTS OF WOMAN: AMAZON, MOTHER, MADONNA, COURTESAN

1. "Structural Forms of the Feminine Psyche" by Toni Wolff was first read in 1934 in the Psychological Club in Zurich, and a more detailed version of it in 1948 at the C. G. Jung Institute in Zurich. The paper does not appear in print until 1951 in *Der Psychologe,* Heft 7/8; Herausgeber: Dr. Phil., G. H. Graber, Bern.

2. William Glasser, *Reality Therapy: A New Approach to Psychiatry* (New York: Harper & Row, 1965), p. 6.

3. Sylvia Plath, *The Bell Jar* (New York, Harper & Row, 1971).

CRISIS IN THE MADONNA: NO LONGER A LADY

1. Srully Blotnick, *Otherwise Engaged: The Personal Lives of Successful Career Women* (New York: Facts on File, 1985), p. 206.

2. Marion Woodman, *Addiction to Perfection: The Still Unravished Bride* (Toronto: Inner City Books, 1982), pp. 182–185.

3. Rosemary Daniell, *Sleeping with Soldiers: In Search of the Macho Man* (New York: Holt, Rinehart and Winston, 1985), p. 152.

4. Irene Claremont de Castillejo, *Knowing Woman* (New York: Harper & Row, 1973), pp. 110–111.

5. Betty Friedan, *The Feminine Mystique* (New York: W. W. Norton, 1962).

EMBRACING FEMININITY: MELTING THE AMAZON ARMOR

1. William Shakespeare, *The Taming of the Shrew* (New York: Penguin, 1981).

2. Carol Orsborn, *Enough Is Enough: Exploding the Myth of Having It All* (New York: G. P. Putnam's Sons, 1986).

3. Matina Horner, "Femininity and Successful Achievement: A Basic Inconsistency," Chap. 3 in Bardwick, Douvan, Horner, and Gutmann, eds., *Feminine Personality and Conflict* (Belmont, Calif: Brooks/

Col, 1970); "Why Bright Women Fear Success," in *The Female Experience*, from the Editors of *Psychology Today* (Del Mar, Calif.: CRM, 1973).

4. Irene Claremont de Castillejo, *Knowing Woman* (New York: Harper & Row, 1973).

5. Eric Berne, *Transactional Analysis in Psychotherapy* (New York: Grove Press, 1961).

FINDING YOUR HERO: MAGNETIZING YOUR MAN

1. M. Esther Harding, *The Way of All Women* (New York: Harper & Row, 1970), p. 36.

2. Eric Berne, *Games People Play* (New York: Random House, 1964), p. 112.

3. Sylvia Ann Hewlett, *A Lesser Life: The Myth of Women's Liberation in America* (New York: William Morrow, 1986).

4. *The Wall Street Journal*, February 11, 1982.

5. Marion Woodman, *Addiction to Perfection: The Still Unravished Bride* (Toronto: Inner City Books, 1982), p. 7.

6. Francine Klagsbrun, *Married People: Staying Together in the Age of Divorce* (New York: Bantam Books, 1985).

7. Robert A. Johnson, *We: Understanding the Psychology of Romantic Love* (New York: Harper & Row, 1983).

8. Hewlett, op. cit., p. 179.

9. Woodman, op. cit., p. 52.

10. C. G. Jung, *Civilization in Transition*, Vol. 10 of *The Collected Works of C. G. Jung* (Princeton, N.J.: Princeton University Press, Bollingen Series 20, 1964), par. 260.

11. Irene Claremont de Castillejo, *Knowing Woman: A Feminine Psychology* (New York: Harper & Row, 1973), p. 116.

12. John Sanford, *The Invisible Partners* (New York: Paulist Press, 1980), p. 19.

13. Marie-Louise Von Franz, *Puer Aeternis* (Santa Monica, Calif.: Sigo Press, 1970), p. 1.

14. Ovid, *Metamorphosis*, with an English translation by James Justus Miller. 2 vols. (London and Cambridge, Mass.: Loeb Classic Library, 1946).

15. Dan Kiley, *The Peter Pan Syndrome* (New York: Avon, 1983).

16. Susan Littwin, *The Postponed Generation* (New York: William Morrow, 1986), p. 15.

17. Hervey Cleckley, *The Mask of Sanity* (New York: NAL, 1982).

18. Harding, op. cit., p. 55.

19. De Castillejo, op. cit., p. 83.

MANAGING MEN: HANDLING YOUR HERO AND MAKING HIM YOURS

1. Lasch, Christopher, *The Culture of Narcissism: American Life in an Age of Diminishing Expectations* (New York: Warner Books, 1979), p. 343.

2. Florida Scott-Maxwell, *Women and Sometimes Men* (New York: Alfred A. Knopf, 1957), p. 47.

3. Marion Woodman, *Addiction to Perfection: The Still Unravished Bride* (Toronto: Inner City Books, 1982), p. 122.

4. Mary Renault, *The Bull from the Sea* (New York: Pantheon, 1962), p. 159.

5. Eric Berne, *Transactional Analysis in Psychotherapy* (New York: Grove Press, 1961).

SWEET SURRENDER: BODY AND SOUL

1. Mary Renault, *The Bull from the Sea* (New York: Pantheon, 1962), p. 139.

2. Ibid., p. 134.

3. Ibid., p. 140.

4. Ibid., p. 154.

5. Marion Woodman, *Addiction to Perfection: The Still Unravished Bride* (Toronto: Inner City Books, 1982), p. 85.

6. Ibid., p. 88.

7. Ibid., p. 91.

8. William Shakespeare, *The Taming of the Shrew* (New York: Penguin, 1981), p. 119.

9. Ibid., p. 120

10. Ibid.

11. Ibid., p. 139.

12. Ibid.

13. Woodman, op. cit., p. 124.

AMAZON LADY: FULFILLING YOUR FEMININITY
THROUGH MARRIAGE

1. Irene Claremont de Castillejo, *Knowing Woman: A Feminine Psychology* (New York: Harper & Row, 1973), p. 105.

2. Mary Renault, *The Bull from the Sea* (New York: Pantheon, 1962), p. 220.

DR. TONI GRANT is a distinguished clinical psychologist and a pioneer in media psychology. In 1975, she revolutionized her field with the advent of the "Dr. Toni Grant Program" on ABC Radio, a psychology call-in format, which quickly achieved a devoted following and was subsequently syndicated nationally.

Dr. Grant's academic credentials include a B.A. in English literature from Vassar College and an M.S. and Ph.D. in clinical psychology from Syracuse University. She has been the recipient of many honors and awards for public service, among them a 1976 National Media Award from the American Psychological Association, a Distinguished Service Award from the Group Psychotherapy Association of Southern California, and a Learned Research Journal Award from Brandeis University.

Dr. Grant is recently married to John Bell, industrialist and financier. They live in Beverly Hills, California, with their four children.

If you would like to share a Success Story with Dr. Toni Grant, you can write to her at the following address:

Dr. Toni Grant
c/o John Bell Enterprises
3460 Wilshire Boulevard
Suite 909
Los Angeles, California 90010